ORDINARY LIVES

edited by

CLIVE MURPHY

Clive Murphy

1 The Good Deeds of a Good Woman
by BEATRICE ALI
The memoirs of a former street character

2 Born to Sing
by ALEXANDER HARTOG
The memoirs of an East End mantle presser

In preparation:

3 Four Acres and a Donkey
by S. A. B. ROGERS
The memoirs of a lavatory attendant

4 Love, Dears
by MARJORIE GRAHAM
The memoirs of a former chorus girl

The author of *Born to Sing*, the second autobiography in my series, *Ordinary Lives*, was the loudest, most provocative talker in 'Georgina's', an East End café I frequented during Autumn, 1973. One night I approached his table, dared suggest he use my tape-recorder to make a book. I was a total stranger: that he agreed to embark on the venture without a moment's apparent hesitation surprised me. But Alex Hartog—tenor, mantle presser, pundit and mini Job—is a very surprising person.

EDITOR

BORN TO SING

Alexander Hartog

BORN TO SING

Recorded November 1973 to July 1974

LONDON : DENNIS DOBSON

First published in Great Britain 1978 by
Dobson Books Ltd, 80 Kensington Church Street, London, W8

Printed in Great Britain by
Bristol Typesetting Co, Ltd,
Barton Manor, St Philips, Bristol

ISBN 0 234 72037 9

To my most loyal supporter and admirer
my mother

ONE

I've never since the day my mother died had that feeling of somebody loves me, somebody cares for me, there's somebody to come home to. Anything I asked for as a kid she invariably gave me. I never had to count the cost because I never had to pay. She tried to make my life as full and rich as possible within the means of the family.

She never wasted anything. Everything was re-cycled. My brothers' clothes—at one time I was the proud possessor of six suits, four pairs of shoes, four overcoats and two double-breasted waistcoats. Food—when the milk went off, instead of throwing it away, she waited four or five days until it turned into a jelly, then she took a raw onion and a cucumber, sliced them into small cubes, added a touch of salt, mixed in the milk-jelly and served it to us with brown bread for our tea. Delicious!

She was the best cook I ever sat down to table with. Her Lancashire hot-pot, her bowls and bowls of calf's feet jellies, her chopped herrings, her borsht and cinnamon, her apple strudel and cinnamon, her fried plaice . . . Oh, her fried plaice! There was a whole procedure. First she heated some oil in a frying-pan till it sang with small bubbles. Then she wet the fish in salt water and put it into the white of egg—flop, flop. Then she put it into matzo meal—flop, flop. Then she put it into the pan, and there was a sizzle and little sparks of flame used to jump up and a skin formed around the fish, delicate and crispy while, inside, the meat was soft and tender.

Instead of running out to play, I would sometimes watch her on a Friday morning preparing the food for the week. It was a pleasure and an education to see her de-gut a hen, chop it into pieces—the fliegels, the poulkas—stuff the neck with sage, onion and spices and sew it up with white cotton, divide the breasts into two, take the gall out of the stomach, sort the egg, the liver, then, after taking the yellow fat from the rump and frying it into a liquid which she put into an earthenware bowl to be used for frying, put everything else in a gallon pot for boiling and making into delicacies. In her last two years, when I was trying to entice her to eat, I was able to return the pleasure by cooking her the dishes that I had enjoyed as a boy—boiled chicken, chopped meat casseroles with baked potatoes and rice, soufflés . . . For the soufflés I added a touch of butter to some eggs in a pure steel frying-pan, and I whipped, whipped and whipped them with a fork into a fluffy mountain. She lapped it up.

I don't think it was because I was a namby-pamby that I was so fond of my mother. It was more because the real essential part of the Jewish religion is not in the Synagogue, which is a place to suffer in, but in the home where children have their character built and learn, through the festivals, holidays and little prayers and little traditions, about their history and religion. It's a warm, gay, happy, friendly atmosphere, very thick, no shackles. I've never met it in any other people except the Italians. When a child says something clever or amusing, the mother doesn't say, 'Shut up! I'm trying to do something!', she rejoices, she shares in the intelligence, the wit, then, when the occasion arises, she explains that we eat brown bopkes and red beans during Purim because of this cracking Jewish girl called Esther who helped to overcome Haman, a Hitler in Ancient Babylon; that we drink wine at Passover to remind us we are no longer slaves, and that matzos began when the Jews were told to take a walk out of Egypt and hadn't time to put bread with yeast in it into their saddle-bags; that the boiled eggs which we eat with the matzos are mixed in salt water to celebrate the crossing of the Red Sea, and that bitter herbs are to remind us of the bitter herbs of oppression.

Jews live for their children. Grown-ups go without to give them food, clothes, education. They believe that it's in their children that they live on. That's why I regret that I'm a single man. I look after my sister, Betty, because her children in a small way will be my perpetuation. Sometimes I hear people say they didn't ask to be born. Crap! Don't let anyone try to tell me they didn't enjoy letting their mother cuddle them and wash and powder them, and their father carry them on his shoulders and play with them, that they didn't enjoy having sweeties from their parents and they didn't like having a dog and a cat! Even when you're grown up and you've had to accept that what happens to you is a matter of your own endeavour and that sometimes your own endeavour without luck isn't enough, you can still enjoy life. Just opening my eyes every morning gives me pleasure. And, if it's a nice day and not too bloody cold, I like getting out of bed and, when I'm dressed, I can't wait to get down to the café and get a cup of tea in me. It's all to be enjoyed. Every bit.

I cannot over-stress the fact that my mother was the most important person in my life. She was not formally educated, but she had a very sharp brain and an appreciation of beauty. She was born in Lithuania. Her father, according to what she told me, was a very big man with a beard and a bass voice. He was a farmer and an interior decorator, an artistic farmer you might say! Where now you put a border on a wall with a strip of paper, he would paint it on, floral designs and all. His farm was just outside Vilna, and he married a woman about five foot from another village and they had a large family—four or five daughters, including my mother, Chaya, and two sons. They were noted singers in the region. Whenever there was a banquet for bigwigs or a marriage, they were always invited because people enjoyed listening to his basso profundo and her delicate, high, soprano voice.

A match was made for my mother, a true love match, with a Jewish boy, the boy of her dreams. But in about 1905 he was called up with one of her brothers to the Japanese-Russian War, and neither of them ever came back. So she was left a widow with a little boy, my elder brother, Jacob, Jacob Fedder. She packed her bag and, with the instinct of all persecuted people to keep moving till they find somewhere peaceful where they're not spat at, she went through Russia, Poland, Germany, France, working as a cook, till in 1908 she reached London. On the boat from France to England someone dropped five sovereigns in a handkerchief onto the deck. My brother, Jacob—Jack of blessed memory, who died of cancer in 1950 at the age of forty-eight—picked up the handkerchief and took it to his mother who tucked it in her bosom as her stake for when she got to London. Because of those God-given sovereigns she was able to open up a little stall in the Narrow Ways, Petticoat Lane in the East End, selling pins and elastic, and our family remained in business there for nearly fifty years. My mother used to tell us how Jack, even at the age of five, went into the Lane at four or five every morning and put down a couple of orange boxes and a small board. That was her pitch. When the Inspector came along, she would give him threepence, or whatever it was, and get her slip of paper to show she was in business for the day.

A window repairer called Myer Bergwein who came from Vilna ten years earlier found my mother a couple of rooms in the Drum Court, a small court off the Whitechapel Road. Within six months of living there with her little son, Jack, a match was made for her to marry a teacher of Hebrew named Kutner. Someone said to him, 'Look, she's only twenty-one, she's a good-looking woman and she's got a business in the Lane!'

Kutner was—and I say so with all true intention—an egotistical, overbearing bastard. Because he was a scholar and could teach Hebrew, he thought he was better than my mother. He was a snob. And he was mean. The story goes that, when she had been married to him for about a year, he gave her sixpence and said he wanted her to buy half a chicken, a small twill of tea, some sugar and four pounds of potatoes, and expected tuppence change! He was the father of her four sons—Moysha who became Maurice; Zussman who became Cecil and then Steve; Ruben who became Reggie; and Aaron who became Alan. While my mother kept the family by working on the stall, he lost touch with reality and wouldn't teach.

Now my mother couldn't stand a parasite. Same with me. That's why I've got no time for hippies or grown-up students. They're parasites, they're evading the issue. There are some of them who may go on due to brainpower, but ninety per cent plus will never be more nor less than working people who should get out of the studio or get out of the university and go and earn their keep . . . As I was saying, my mother was not a woman to be imposed upon. The marriage died. She kicked her husband out and, after the divorce, found another one, Joseph Hartog, father of me and my sister, Betty. His family name had once been Den Hartog. 'Den' was a Dutch title. It was given originally to a Hartog towards the end of the eighteenth century for entertaining the King by telling stories. 'Den' in Dutch means 'Once upon a time'.

Joseph Hartog was apprenticed for four or five years to a Belgian bamboo chair manufacturer in the East End and then, on reaching the age of twenty, the point when he could demand a man's wages, the manufacturer, discouraged when he couldn't make his way with bamboo in England, returned to Belgium taking the trade with him. My father, after tobacco farming for eight or nine years in Canada, returned to the East End and, at the time he met my mother—who had moved into No. 2, Palmer Street, a house with six or eight rooms, all for the princely sum of seven shillings, or seven and six, a week—was a shlepper, helping on the barrows, and in a pub as a potman. My sister, Betty, was born in October, 1920, and I was born in July, 1922. I can never catch that year and nine months up!

But—*'Out!!'* I was only one year old when there was another parting of the ways. What my mother minded was that, because she was making enough on the stall to take care of him and the whole family, a man of forty didn't seem to be bothering to bring home a couple of bob a week to show that he was trying. She thought he was another parasite. I never saw him again till I was twenty-four or twenty-five and just out of the army. I went to see Betty and he was with her on a visit from the workhouse. He was doddering. He was an old man. He was still angry that my mother had got rid of him. He tried to explain how, being busy with the stall, she didn't pick up a paper, how she didn't realize that between the wars, if you were just a muscleman like he was, you could be hired and fired in a couple of hours; if someone came along and said he'd do your job for a few bob cheaper you were out on your ear; even proud men with trades were begging for any sort of work. I understood him better, but I wished I had my mother's looks. Unfortunately I looked just like he did. I even had his Roman nose!

My mother was beautiful. She had me when she was about

forty, so I only saw her when she was mature. She had a proud, if troubled, face with Slavic features—high cheekbones, bright, dark brown eyes and jet black hair. Her top lip was rather too fine, but her lower one was full. She was five foot one or two, and she was plump with a big pair of breasts. Her cheeks had a rosy bloom. She wore her hair piled up in a bun at the back of her head and, once a week, she used to pull out the pins and it used to drop down to below her backside. She wore a silk shawl with a flattened bracelet that kept it in place. She was influenced not by the fashions of the mid-twenties but by the Alexandrian period with its long dresses and rich colours, purple and deep blue. She wore a whalebone corset when she went out, and bootees she did up by connecting the hooks and eyes. Her nose was little, pert and turned up. Her teeth were not her best feature. In those days you had good teeth more by good luck than anything as dental care wasn't practised extensively. Her skin was of a very fine texture; in fact, when she was eighty, she didn't have any wrinkles on her face or neck, her skin was like creamy white porcelain, and her hair, apart from one or two grey hairs which she never plucked out, was the same colour as when I was a little boy, and her back was as muscular and firm as that of a woman in her thirties. There was something, though, she *did* pass on to me—her strength. Her hand was as big and as strong as a man's. She would tell the story of how her father used to give her a copeck and she used to close her hand and the strongest man in the village couldn't open it up to take the copeck from her.

About 1924, Palmer Street was knocked down and we moved to a house in a court off the Narrow Ways. On one side of the court entrance was a shoe shop called Goodman's. On the other side was Ostwind's, a baker's shop and restaurant. I was disappointed our court hadn't got a pump—kids and dogs love pumps. Anyway, there we lived in a matchbox of a house in the casbah of the East End where there was no such thing as coldness, no lost little boys, and everyone—Jews, Irish, Italians, Scotch—were friendly and noisy and knew that the Hartogs had a little boy who liked to walk away from his mother and would say, if I was two hundred yards from home—and two hundred yards, even a hundred yards, is a long way for a baby—'Hello! You lost?' and take me back to her.

There was only one person I was afraid of in the court, and he was a little Jewish man with a head as big as the moon. I was coming home one day with my brother, Alan. This man was standing there. I stopped. Alan said, 'Come on, Alex!' I wouldn't move! My brother walked past him, keeping on the pavement. I went right round the block so that I could come home from the other side. Later, when I was sixteen or seventeen, I saw the same man and I said to myself, 'I was right. He *is* repulsive.' He was a squat four foot ten. The circumference of his head was at least thirty-five inches and he had a yellowish complexion and big staring eyes and big heavy lids.

By the time I was three and my sister five, the Petticoat Lane, Commercial Street, Whitechapel and Commercial Road up to New Road were known to us. For us that *was* the East End, and it was all home. If we went too far, a good Jew or a good Irishman would give us a penny and put us on a bus. My mother knew that while she worked we wouldn't come to any harm. She let us walk around and play while she made business. A big Jewish woman with a florid complexion, Mrs Ellis who sold flowers off a barrow down Toynbee Street, called us the Bisto Kids. Sometimes she used to take out a bag and give us a sweet each. Then there was Mrs Cohen, with a restaurant in Old Castle Street, who made us welcome at three o'clock with a cup of tea and a chocolate éclair. We played with her son, Sidney, till my mother packed up and came for us at about five. My mother was known to many people. A cup of tea, a small meal, a word of advice, a few shillings—we had a regular procession of people she brought home for the comfort of talking to somebody. She was haimisher (homely) like many Jewish women. Mrs Lewis was a very old friend of hers. She used to come to our house on a Saturday when mother could relax. She was sad and dumpy and wore a hat with a wide brim with one side going up and the other down. She always brought me little china knick-knacks —trees, cats, cows, mother dogs and puppies, mother elephants and baby elephants. She never brought anything for Betty, maybe because Betty was getting plenty of attention from the window repairer, Myer Bergwein who regarded me as just an unwanted little burden, maybe because Betty didn't sing for her like I did. I was always singing. Many a time someone bunged me a penny to sing them a song, not 'Baa Baa Black Sheep' but songs like 'Who Were You With Last Night?'. According to my mother, I was singing to myself three months after I was born. In fact, I was taught by a very small and high soprano voice that sang in my head to me at night before I fell asleep.

The Jewish Infants' School had two entrances—one in Commercial Street and another in a court down the Narrow Ways where a Dutch firm sold cigars and the police used to put their capes. Betty and I used to play in this court and, one morning come about ten to nine when she had to go to school, she went upstairs. Well—I was only two and a half—I didn't know she was going to school, all I knew was my sister was going away from me. I climbed up the stairs after her calling, 'Betty! Betty! Betty!', and followed her into a room and was taken by her teacher into another room, a nursery with kids a year or so older than me where we sat on the floor and played with plasticine and bricks and, during the last hour, lay down and had a sleep.

That was how I started at the Jewish Infants' School at two and a half, and I stayed there till I was seven. To me the teachers, young and middle-aged, were all beautiful. They were friendly and considerate, all the nice things of life. A year or two ago I used to eat in a café called 'Rosie's' in Whitechapel. The owner's daughter was six or seven. She was very nervous, spoilt and wouldn't eat. She used to sit down opposite me, and I used to talk to her, tell her jokes and stories. One evening we were talking about something or other and I said, half joke, half serious, 'I'm beautiful.' A man across the way wanted to be funny. He said, '*You're* beautiful?!' I said, 'All right. *I* won't say it. Just ask the little girl.' And she said, 'Yes, he's beautiful.' To a child it's not the appearance, the height, the lines, it's what comes across when another person communicates with feelings. And to her I was beautiful, and to me my teachers were beautiful.

I was reading and writing by the age of five so as to keep up with a boy called Sidney Conrich who was the same age. When I couldn't tell the time and found Sidney could, I very soon could tell the time too! The brain was just like blotting paper. We now sat at miniature desks on miniature chairs, twenty to twenty-five little people. In the winter, a blazing coal fire burned in the grate with an enormous guard in front of it. The walls were covered with drawings, paintings and designs. I remember taking a light-brown piece of paper about ten by eight inches and with a piece of yellow chalk I drew a monkey sitting down. My teacher, Miss Solomons, put it on the wall to encourage me.

I was a greedy guzzler. Every other kid had a half pint bottle of milk. I had two because my mother used to give me a penny instead of a halfpenny. I drank every drop. Just outside school there was an old Indian who sold Indian toffee at a halfpenny a twill. I always liked his toffee better than anybody else's because it was broken up into uneven pieces. At the back of the Jewish Free School nearby there was a Negro with a tray of liquorice and nuts. A little further on, a dwarf sat in a chair outside a shop where his two sisters sold home-made toffee at two ounces for a halfpenny with little bits of coconut on it and a lemony flavour.

For tuppence or threepence school dinners were very, very nice. We sat in a hall made out of classrooms with the partitions pushed back. My two favourites were the Spotted Dick, which is plum duff with raisins in, and the College Pudding with syrup over it. There was a time when, as an adult, I went purposely into English restaurants and put up with things like roast beef so as to have the Spotted Dick or the College Pudding at the end! We were very, very happy, boys and girls talking together. Later, evil people tried to separate us. I believed then, and I believe now, that boys and girls, men and women, think the same. There shouldn't be any mystery.

Outside school if you were hungry all you had to do was knock on a door and walk in. Out of a population of three hundred thousand in Stepney, about a hundred and twenty thousand, a third, were Jewish. Most of them now have moved out to Golders Green and Stamford Hill, and those that are left have lost the Yiddishkeit to help one another. It's a surface thing now, but in those days you cared deeply about your friends and relations and co-religionists. Before the war there was a camaraderie, a warm feeling you would never starve, and, never mind about the Kitchen in Butler Street being Jewish, everybody went there, Jew and Gentile, and you didn't even have to have a bowl or a plate, just bring a tin, and the soup was thick with meat and vegetables. I remember going to that Kitchen, *and* to the Joneses in Artillery Lane who had cows, and you brought your billy-can and asked for a ha'p'orth of milk which they ladled for you with a jug from a churn. For chickens you went to the stalls—sixpence a pound, the best. The narrow streets and the dirty little homes and covered alleyways were cramped, there wasn't an inch of territory wasted, with each door you walked past leading to a court, but the people were friendly, and religion or race seemed to mean nothing.

Imagine my surprise when we moved over to Bermondsey and there was a different atmosphere! We were in Stroud House, a Council block near Golden Lane, and I was an infant traveller, a commuter between there and the school and the court where my mother kept her stock. I had thought that if you treated people nice and friendly they would treat you nice in the same way. As I've already said, I was born in a friendly neighbourhood where everybody knew everybody else and there were no enemies and there was no difference between colour and race—Jew, Gentile, Scotch, Irish, Welsh, Italian—and people in the main were hardworking and they wouldn't let you starve and, if there wasn't an institution to do it, they would give you a cup of tea or a sandwich. I assumed it was the same all the way over. It wasn't.

The daily routine was this. Betty and I set out by bus from Golden Lane with my mother and Jack, or one of my other brothers, at about seven in the morning. We got to the Lane about ten to eight, went to a court off Old Castle Street where Betty and I watched the stock being put by my mother and brother into the compartments and onto the top of our stall which was a solid affair, a three foot cube with a board over it about four foot square, like a giant box on wheels. We then all pushed the stall out into the Narrow Ways where my mother and brother made a proper show of baby lace, curtain lace, buttons, pins, elastic, hooks and eyes, buckles, belts, many, many bits and pieces housewives wanted. (She changed to cardigans in the late twenties and then went into the fruit and salad game after the embargo on German goods in 1933.) At about eight-thirty we went into Old Castle Street to Mrs Cohen's and had a cup of tea and a cheese sandwich. Then my sister and me went to the Jewish Infants' School where we stayed till three-thirty. After that we went wandering and ended up at Mrs Cohen's to be collected by my mother to go home at five.

Because I was a much travelled little boy I was friendly at Stroud House with the people across the landing and on top of us and below us. Around midday, one Saturday morning, I was playing with a little boy about four, my own age. He was showing me what his uncle could do with a couple of potatoes, sticking matchsticks here and there to make them into animals. All of a sudden I heard a voice, a man's voice, and the boy looked up and said, 'Hello, Uncle! Show us how you make an animal!' The uncle began to give a demonstration and, as he explained, he was talking out of nowhere about 'him' and how 'he' was a Jew and not a Roman Catholic, not a Christian. It was as if he was trying to teach his nephew the evils of the Jews without frightening him. He was bland. He was careful not to come out with the essentials. I was looking at him in wide-eyed wonder. I was watching him putting in all the matchsticks with his agile hands and asking myself why he was talking about foreigners and dirty people that come into the district. He was hinting. He was looking at his nephew and, while he put in the matchsticks, he said, 'Tomorrow, you'll be going to church, won't you? Not like some people I know!' He was trying to create a wall. 'I don't know where they come from. They're not clean like us. They're certainly not British.' He was teaching the boy anti-Semitism.

Prejudiced people can inflict enormous harm on little children. Early on in a Jew's life, he learns that some people don't like him and that he's got something special. That boy never spoke to me again. At the age of four I found that there was a gap between 'Them' and 'Us'.

Luckily as a young boy there was a different sort of 'Them' and 'Us' to make up for it, the 'Them' and 'Us' of the Petticoat Lane and of Butler Street, now Brune Street, where, to save constant travel to and from the market, my mother was given a Council flat a year later in Carter House, the ground floor, No. 18. 'Us' was not only me, my sister, my brothers and my mother, it was all the people living round about, and the hucksters, the con men, the spielers. The tourists, the one-day traffic merchants, were 'Them'.

The feeling I had—and it didn't go away throughout my youth—was that the Lane was a carnival. There was a man who sold ointment to cure corns. He didn't have any corns himself but he'd put some ointment on the side of his hand and say if you wrapped it in a bandage you could peel off the corn like the skin of an onion in the morning. People bought and nobody came back. Another man sold what he said was extract of Spanish Fly—'Don't give it to minors! It'll make them into men and women before they leave school!' He had as a come-on a strong-man with a heap of rubber expander-sets he was for ever threatening to pull but never did. I've got an idea they were related! Another man sold home-made boot polish, another—I don't think he made a fortune at it—you could buy double envelopes from him, put something in one end, turn it round and make it disappear. One man used to cut off two- or three-inch lengths of bitter herbs, charge two or threepence a time and say they were good for piles, loose bowels, pimples, tell you the whole story. There were four or five from the First World War, and one of them turned a barrel-organ while the rest in ladies' dresses did ballet, tap. Prince Monolulu, wearing a feather head-dress, would say, 'I've got a horse!' and, if there were sixteen runners in a race, he would have sixteen horses to tell you for sixpence apiece. There was Little Ginger, the Strong Man. Apart from the conventional tricks of breaking chains and bending bars, he once for a bet, and it was only a cup of tea, bent a penny with his fingers. There was a unique act, a father first of all and then his son. He used to swallow glass and coal and brick and then plead for a bit of financial appreciation. There was a boy ventriloquist with the true trick of a showman. He said, 'Get back two or three yards! If you're too near me I won't be able to breathe properly!' A man used to sling a whole lot of crockery up in the air and shout, 'Thirty bob!' as he caught it. Most of these old time performers are up in Leeds now. An old Jamaican woman had a birdcage with a canary in it and hundreds of little printed pink slips. She'd ask what month you were born, then tap her stick on the perch and the bird would pick up a pink slip and that was yours for a penny. I found out that I was going to be married three times and have seven children. I want my money back.

A very plausible Welshman with a good speaking voice did a mind-reading act. He bandaged a girl's eyes and asked her questions about people he pointed to. A long time afterwards, just after the war, in fact, when I was about twenty-five, I came across him working the same act in the West End with another girl. He pointed to me and asked me did I want to ask her anything. Very quietly I asked him to ask her would I succeed in my ambition. She said, 'No', and that came true.

TWO

My ambition, always, was to become a professional singer. I wonder if it had anything to do with that small singing voice I heard as a baby. Was it one of my family ancestors within me? Although the Jewish religion is not supposed to believe in reincarnation, I do. I was born with a singing technique that grew with my voice. I always knew what I was going to be. I knew it! Everyone used to say, 'Oh what a marvellous voice he's got!' In the Infants' School I was singing. Everywhere singing! And in those days singing was appreciated. If you stood up and did a warble, people didn't applaud politely because you were a kid or a bit of a character. People judged you, and only if you had anything special did they encourage you. When I was seven or eight my brother, Ruby, began taking me to the Sunday Concerts of the Workers' Circle in Great Alie Street. He polished my shoes, put my tie straight and dragged me along. There was always a couple of singers, a violinist and a pianist. Some singers had arrived, some were coming. The audience—mostly Jewish people—applauded those that were coming even more than the rest. By God, they used to applaud! They used to make them feel, 'This is it! This is one more step on the road!'

My family was not a religious family but, when I went to the Jewish Free School at the age of eight, my mother began sending me on Monday, Tuesday, Wednesday and Thursday nights and Sunday afternoons to the Talmud Torah—that's the Hebrew classes—because she wanted me to be able to read the prayers. I'd finish school at ten to four, go and have something to eat and, at quarter to six, I'd be at the Brick Lane Talmud Torah, the Brick Lane School of Hebrew on top of the Synagogue.

There I met Sidney Rosenthal, the son of the Beadle of Duke's Place Synagogue. He was eight years old, the same as me, and invited me home to tea one day to meet his family. Well, during tea, Alex was talking, but Alex was also cocking an ear, for Alex had a habit of cocking ears and isolating one thing from another. Alex heard a big voice, a big tenor voice, a big free-wheeling voice being practised three floors below. It was the voice of the chazzen, the cantor Kusavitsky, who used to sing at the Dalston Synagogue and had come to Duke's Place to be its principal chazzen. He could do trills and runs and could take top C's and D's in full voice, a Caruso with guts. You could hear Kusavitsky's big, brown, fantastic voice ten streets away. It was a voice that had power. His older brother—and I heard both of them together after the war—had the fine art, a lyrical quality nearer to Gigli, but I preferred the younger one, the one I heard that afternoon when I was eight at Duke's Place, the voice which told me that, though I was a singer born, I had something to learn and also something to aim for. It was as if I had been assigned a task.

In the same year, by pure accident, I came across a choir directed by a Mr Mellows in the ground floor hall under the Jewish Library, Mulberry Street, which performed in the Great Hall at the Jewish Free School for the High Holidays. I happened to hear singing as I passed, so I went in, and there were these men and boys practising for the Rosh Hashanah, the New Year holiday, and Yom Kippur, the Day of Atonement, the day the Arabs were to attack the Jews in 1973, the one day a Jew will not bear arms. I was allowed to join. There wasn't a register, but those of us who carried on for the two months of rehearsal had a nosh up at Lyons Coventry Street Corner House and then a pantomime with plenty of chocolates and ice creams.

During Rosh Hashanah and Yom Kippur you had to be in the Synagogue all day singing with the cantors, superlative showmen rendering their own versions of the prayers and putting in their own tunes and melodies like Jolsons and opera singers combined. On Yom Kippur I saw something that changed my life. I saw two old men drop down dead because they didn't eat that day. It was after that part of the service where we bang our breasts and say, 'We have sinned, we have sinned, we have sinned.' We're liars but we're confessing just in case. I told my mother when I came home. I said, 'Mammeleben, I'm not going to fast.' I had seen two good men who were innocent of any crime just drop down and die. I never fasted again and I won't fast now.

That day I was also able to see from the height of the stage a scene which no Gentile or unorthodox Jew ever sees, and that is the scene on that one day of the year, Yom Kippur, when orthodox Jews in Europe pray as the Jews prayed hundreds of years ago. Two or three men are chosen because they are very pious and very learned, and they put on a shawl called a tallith and a cappel which is a little skull-cap and they take their shoes off and kneel on the floor and—protected by a four square group looking out at the congregation and chosen for their size, their strength and their courage to protect these revered men of learning—they pray to God, not from the Book but from the soul. They don't just say the prayers, they wail them.

That same year I also joined the Habonim which you might say is the junior section of the Young Zionists which in turn is the junior section of the Zionists which is divided into those that talk about going to Israel and those that actually go. After supper one evening, I walked round the corner from Carter House into Bell Lane and up to Middlesex Street. I crossed over to Goulston Street, thinking in my little mind, 'Maybe I'll go up to the top of Aldgate and then come back again', when, who do I see coming out of the Goulston Street Buildings but Maxie Cohen, a friend of mine at the Jewish Free. So we're walking and talking. I'm just walking around, but he's walking with a purpose, he's going to the Habonim, to the Joseph Trumpeldor Group which was in the basement of the Duke's Place Synagogue, the Sol Sieff Hall. So I've nothing to do, I go down with him, and they're learning a few Hebrew songs and they're playing with bricks and they're talking about Israel. So I joined the Habonim and I stayed with it right up to the war, and all because by chance I met my old pal, Maxie Cohen.

The Habonim was founded to teach us about Israel, its agriculture and its politics. But things were kept more on the light side for the youngsters—making bricks out of cardboard, for instance, and covering them with plain paper and ornamenting them with Hebrew motifs, then building a house, the symbol of the group. We also went to camp at Christchurch and Herne Bay, on land owned by amicable English farmers. Very nice. We always had cornflakes for breakfast and, during the day, we learned Hebrew and were told stories about the settlers in Israel and their problems. We would play a game of cricket or football, or maybe go down to the beach or to the river for a swim or to climb the little hills. Often different groups would put on little plays or mimes to entertain the others. To entertain is part of the Jewish character. After we had our evening meal and it got dark, there was always the camp fire, and all of us—boys and girls from London, Manchester, Glasgow, Leeds, Birmingham—used to congregate around it and sing and dance the hora in a tight circle, arms around one another's shoulders, rotating, first slowly, then taking off, faster and faster as the songs and the mood took you, the left foot forward and the right foot back, the left foot forward and the right foot back, whirling at such a pace that you were usually more suspended than on the ground. We were a large family. If there wasn't love, there was rapport, there was a feeling of oneness. We were dedicated. We were thinking of Jews going back to Israel and living on a kibbutz. Sensible things filled our minds. When I was fourteen or fifteen, I had a weird experience. One last night, before breaking camp, about a dozen of us—boys and girls—went to a pub and had a couple of beers. When I got back at about half past nine, ten o'clock, the camp fire was still roaring and people were singing and dancing. I went into the big tent for a cheese sandwich and some tea. Then the funny thing happened. I was talking to someone, and, before he spoke, I knew what he was going to say. The drinks in the pub had so keyed up my brain that I was receiving messages from *his* brain before he said anything. It was my first experience of ESP. For years after that I wouldn't drink any beer because I knew I'd grow tired of conversations that happened twice.

But back to when I was ten. It was then that I had my first disappointment as a singer. Someone in the Jewish Free School said to me, 'Why not go along and see Mr Joseph?' Mr Joseph had been a master at the school and was now a commercial traveller, but at Play Centre in the evenings he rehearsed Concert Parties, playing the piano himself and changing the lyrics if they were too old or too dirty for the people involved. I went to him and I sang 'I'm dancing with tears in my eyes for the girl in my arms isn't you' and 'I blow through here and the music goes around and around'. He took me on for the next show. Also singing in the show was Sid Cohen, twelve years old and elder brother of my friend, Alec Cohen, who used to sit in the desk just ahead of me, a short, very cheerful boy with black hair and big, black eyes, who had run across the road one day and been knocked down by a tram and killed. Sid was going to sing a comic song written by Mr Joseph, about dreaming he was in a jam factory and eating all the jam, called 'I wish I had those dreams when I was awake'.

I'd been to two or three rehearsals and was enjoying them, when the Brick Lane Talmud Torah sent my mother a letter in Hebrew which she had to take round the corner to a woman who could translate it. It said her boy hadn't turned up this past two weeks, was he ill or something? So my mother said to me, 'What's the matter?' and I explained I was singing in the Concert Party at school. She said, 'You can't do *that*! You've got to go to the evening class. It's coming near the time when they give you your suit!' Every year, the Women's Guild of the Synagogue—not professional do-gooders, but well-meaning, well-doing, practical housewives whose husbands had businesses—asked the teachers to submit names of children who were deprived, and then, just before the High Holidays, we were taken down to a private office on the first floor, one class at a time, and measured for a suit, an overcoat and a pair of shoes or boots, and then, the second or third week in November, before going home on the Thursday night, we were given our separate parcels.

So the Concert Party was one thing I missed, and Mr Joseph took a boy out of the chorus who finished up as a famous pop artist just after the war singing hot numbers like an American, and gave him my songs and said to me, 'I'm sorry. Maybe when you're older.' And where was I? Sitting down in the audience, listening to that amateur punk, wondering to myself, 'My God! What's happened?! Why am I going to Hebrew class?!' I can tell you that, as soon as I was thirteen, I never went back to the class or to the Synagogue! There are things you can't continue. Religion wasn't going to interfere with *my* life.

The frustration! Kids, parents, we all rolled up to this concert on Sunday at six o'clock. We were sat in the Great Hall of the Jewish Free which any theatre man would give his soul for. With its four galleries, it could seat about three thousand. It was enormous—height about a hundred feet, seventy feet long, forty to fifty feet wide. The stage was fifteen to twenty feet deep and ran the entire width of the hall. On this occasion there was a navy blue curtain at the back, and a white and yellow one with a floral design which was dropped for one or two items. But when you come to talent, scenery is superfluous. On stage were about thirty seats, in three or four rows. The boys sat down and sang a few rousing choruses. Then one from here, one from there, did a bit of cross-patter. Then Sid Cohen sang 'I wish I had those dreams when I was awake'. Then this pop-singer-to-be, this future tormentor of housewives' souls, sang my two songs. Thick set. Curly hair. Bright sparkling eyes. He sang them OK but I didn't clap. I was a victim of circumstance. It wasn't that my mother didn't encourage me as a singer. I'm not blaming her. It's just that she had to make a living for six boys and a girl. Apart from her first romance she'd had two layabout husbands and she had to give us food and put the clothes on our back.

The Jewish Free School was in Bell Lane. It was not the kids or teachers that impressed me most, it was the building. I could sense it—a big, warm, friendly mother with the right vibrations. On the boys' side (Seniors and Juniors), block after block after block, spanning four or five periods from about 1820 to 1910, ran and joined and cross-joined and came together at the Girls' School (Seniors and Juniors, which had its own three or four buildings) in the middle at a rounded tuck shop, back of which was a small court which led you to the continuing bigness of the Great Hall. I'd say that the school had at least twelve halls, excluding the Great Hall and the big gymnasium. Oil lamps hoisted on hooks lit one of the yards. Another one had electric switches. Another one was lit by gas. The complex was so big, there were parts of the Girls' School you knew nothing about. Every time there was a break, I could walk down long, narrow passages taking me from an old block into a new block and into big, spacious rooms. No space was wasted. The older boys even ate their meals in a partitioned section of the Great Hall in the main part of which the women teachers played badminton. Even the basements were fantastic. They included a shooting range used once upon a time by the Jewish Lads' Brigade who became soldiers in the Boer and the First World War. Teachers' common rooms were down there, too, and were used by night for discussions and rehearsing Concert Parties. There were toilets there, passages, other rooms running off. It was a beehive. I have a theory that a building develops a personality, almost a life, of its own. When there's nobody in a school, it's sad. As soon as girls and boys are moving around, playing there, it's happy. One morning, about eleven o'clock, two days after the summer holidays had started, I asked the caretaker, Mr Saunders, could I get my rubbers from a cupboard in my classroom. On my way out, I noticed how sad and lonely the school was. Buildings participate in the lives of their occupants and only come alive again when they return.

In term-time the school was used from early morning right up till nine or ten at night. When school came to an end, many of the teachers volunteered to do two or three hours, a couple of evenings a week, to teach the violin, purse making, boot repairing, woodwork, metalwork, pottery, musical appreciation, printing.

Dr Bernstein was the headmaster. He was a Bachelor of Science, a Bachelor of Arts, he had four lines of degrees. You name it, he had it. He even wore a purple sash. He was methodical and had a good memory, but clever people aren't clever all the time. The school had a Parliament. If a boy did something wrong, he was not always brought before the headmaster, but before a panel of boys who used to judge him. I was against it. The judges were just as stupid as the boy they were trying. They had no compassion, no understanding. They were fairer than fair and their idea of fairer than fair was worse than the headmaster's. I told him so. 'Don't get these to do your villainy for you!' I said. Not that *he* didn't punish as well. He was a sadist. When he gave you two strokes of the cane because you were two minutes late in the morning, you couldn't write for two hours. All you could do was put your burning, painful hands on the metal part of the desk to ease the pain. The cane was about an inch thick with a little give. He hit you in such a way that he caught the side of your thumb, on the middle joint, and the tip of your small finger—on both hands, first left, then right. Most of the teachers were not for the cane, they'd sooner give you lines, but Bernstein seemed to love inflicting punishment so there was a Black Book kept in his study which the offending pupil had to call for. A teacher of mine, another sadistic bully called Mr Martin, about thirty years old, a four-eyes who used to sling pieces of chalk at the boys and yet, if they were to put up their hands towards him, he'd run out of the bloody room—he used to send me to find the Black Book regularly so he could enter my name in it. Then I'd join Bernstein's usual quota of about twenty boys that he made wait outside his study till he was ready to cut us up like a butcher.

I had a stammer. As well as the fact I was a sensitive, quick-witted boy whose speaking couldn't match the speed of his thinking, it was caused by a series of accidents. I was running around a room in our flat in Bermondsey when I bumped into my brother, Aaron, who was carrying a mug of boiling tea which he dropped onto my nut. Shortly after that I got on an orange box to see the time on the clock on the mantelpiece, and the box turned and I finished up cracking the back of my head on the grate. Next, when we moved to Carter House, I was trying to empty a bone to make a shofar, and dug the knife between my forefinger and thumb. Just my luck when I was sent from the Infants to the Junior School of the Jewish Free, a hulking brute of thirteen or fourteen from the Seniors called me 'Roscoe Ates' which didn't help. Roscoe Ates was an American comedian who had a stammer when he was young and conquered it and found that he could be a comedian by pretending to have it again. He appeared in films. He'd go 'D-d-d' and change the word. Comedians in this country, too, right up to the late 1950's used to think it was funny to take off a man or a woman with an impediment. I can quote the jokes by heart. They are burned in my brain. Everybody laughed except those with a stammer. *They* used to squirm.

There was a class in the school for boys with an impediment like me. Miss Richardson ran it. She was at least six foot tall, with a long thin nose, a rather thin face, dark brown hair. She was a very sincere, very nice person. She had a theory that the reason why we children had an impediment was we didn't get enough sleep or we didn't know how to relax. She thought we were frustrated or ill-treated and that our parents didn't love us. She wanted us to discuss our problems with one another, she was dropping stones into the water to cause ripples, hoping one or two of us would speak about our unhappiness. But when you get a lot of stammerers together, that doesn't work, so all we used to do in the end was lie on green ground-sheets in this long room of hers on Mondays for two to two and a half hours. We were given red note-books and encouraged to record in them the other times, apart from the normal sleeping hours, when we were able to relax. I wish I could have a conversation with her now. I'd tell her from thirty years' experience of suffering, of being alone in the crowd, of making stupid noises like a baby trying to gargle, that it's nothing to *do* with psychoneurosis, being depressed, being deprived. No. It's due to lack of co-ordination between the brain and the tongue. I've helped many, many people by telling them this. Oh, if only I could have been told the truth as a kid by someone with my hard-earned knowledge! Don't be too aware of the workings of the brain—that defeats your attempts to speak. Keep control of the speed of your tongue. The *tongue* should be leader and curb the pace of the brain's quick thinking. Speak! Do the physical side and the brain will take care of itself. The brain must slow down to the tongue's requirements, not the tongue speed up to the brain's requirements. Whether you're six or sixty, reach a rhythm between the two and you'll be able to do what man has done since he's become a civilized animal, not grunt but communicate. It's so simple but it's true. Work at it! Practise to counteract the bad habit, the warp that's in your mind! If, by saying these words, I can achieve some comfort and cure for the millions of people who suffer from speech defects all over the world, this book will not have been in vain.

I wish all my teachers were as well-meaning as Miss Richardson. Unfortunately I had Mr Martin, another type of sadist who was short and tubby and chewed sweets, but if you brought sweets to school yourself he confiscated them and ate them like a gluttonous pig in front of you. Then there was Mr Cousins, a singer, a choirmaster, an amateur actor who enjoyed enacting bible stories. It was he who suggested to Dr Bernstein that the boys do an hour or so's homework every evening. That man was bloody stupid! All day education was poured into us. Ten to four we wanted out. You don't overwork a young boy's brain! That lasted only about a week, thank God, because the kids were moaning, and parents began to complain and one or two of them sent a deputation to the headmaster.

To my mind, the best two teachers I had were Mr Bourne, my second year teacher, and Mr Rose, my fourth. Though it was ten out of ten for everything else, when I read for the others they used to give me two out of ten because of my impediment. 'All right, Hartog. Two points.' Mr Bourne was a tall, quiet, thin man with a moustache, a gentleman. Without shouting or using the cane, he achieved results. He never used the Black Book. He wasn't an interesting talker but the boys liked him. He wasn't a phoney. He had a commanding presence. He wouldn't begin to speak until the class was quiet. He used a couple of boys as jokes to relax the rest. I was one of them. One day he picked out my habit of pointing to my mouth and cheek when I was startled and he got me to stand out in front of the class and do it again. He only did that once. I didn't resent it. It wasn't done with malice. I think he knew I was doing what a stutterer or a dumb person does when he can't hear what you're saying.

But the man who was the best, even better than Mr Bourne because he was also interesting, was Mr Rose. He was a tall man with a stoop and a very long hooked nose and, as I've said before, when people are nice they're handsome. He realized I had a brain and I could develop and the impediment could be temporary.

I was nearly eleven, the age they picked the scholarship candidates for a rough exam. If they showed that they were good, the girls went on to Raine's and the boys to Davenant. If they failed, it was enough to have been chosen and you were sent to the Central School, a separate entity for boys and girls of high intelligence but not high enough to go elsewhere. Mr Rose realized I wasn't a dummy. I was just a boy with a bit of a nervous complaint. It was morning break. I was behind the board, sharpening my pencil on the sharpener which was attached to the lower part of the cupboard. Mr Rose didn't know I was there. In came Dr Bernstein. 'Mr Rose, I'd like to talk to you for a moment if you're not too busy. I see you've put Hartog down on the Scholarship List. He's a very clever boy but I don't think it's a good idea in view of that impediment.' They walked off to the common room together. Behind the blackboard I cried, no, I bawled my eyes out. Which goes to show that Dr Bernstein was a genius but a fool. The man is dead but may he *not* rest in peace!

Around this time, who should come up to the Brick Lane Talmud Torah one evening on the request, though I didn't know it, of Mr Spector, my teacher there, but Mr Kusavitsky who asked me to sing a song for him. He liked it so much he suggested I join the Tree of Knowledge further up Brick Lane which was for training chazzens of the future. But it wasn't in me. I wasn't a religious boy. I wasn't a frummer. I was for singing in English and to people everywhere, not just in the Synagogue. I wanted fame. I said to Mr Spector, 'That's not for me!'

Now, it is my belief that spirits adopt young children they know have got talent. Talent is not something you acquire. When a baby is born it suffers from an attack of amnesia and so can't remember its former existence. But its talent can't be taken away, its talent as a painter or as a singer or as a musician. It may not know *who* it was in its previous existence but the talent will always remain as part of its nature. I am certain that the spirits surrounding me have always wanted me to be a chazzen. So, when I made the declaration to Mr Spector that I wasn't going to go along with their long laid plans, they decided to punish me. From that point I can say that everything I did in an endeavour to become a professional singer worked against me. I would succeed in some little way, and then, when it came to the crunch, I'd have laryngitis or a headache or the pianist who was supposed to be there wasn't there or the person who was supposed to be giving me a chance decided not to. People all over the East End of London have heard me sing arias and ballads. People who heard me earlier when I was ten and eleven and twelve have said, 'Hello, Alex! How did you get on in your career?' I've had to tell them I got nowhere, and it's because the spirits wanted me to be a chazzen and then, at eleven, there was that deciding moment. I knew instinctively, without accompaniment, how to pitch the voice, and my diction was clear. There had been all the conditioning, all the setting up, from the singing as a baby and as a little boy, from going to the Brick Lane Talmud Torah, from hearing the chazzen, Kusavitsky, in the Duke's Place Synagogue, from joining Mr Mellows' Mulberry Street Choir, from belonging to the Habonim and singing Hebrew songs, to this moment with Mr Spector when I was supposed to say, 'Yes, I'll go to the Tree of Knowledge and become a trainee chazzen. I'll never sing a straight song, but always coloratura. For three or four hours at a time I'll entertain by interpreting songs and prayers that are heard over and over again. And by that I'll achieve some fame in the community. If the young boys who come to the Synagogue with their parents have any voice at all and are a bit religious I'll say, "You don't have to worry about him being a butcher or a farmer or a tailor. Just send him to the school at the Grand Synagogue in Warsaw." ' Nicht für mir! It wasn't enough! It wasn't my scene! I admitted I was born to be a chazzen. The spirits chose my body because it was a strong, healthy body, born of Jewish parents. I had an affinity, I liked to hear the chazzens singing in the Synagogue. But I wanted to be everywhere! At that young age I had already decided in my mind what I wanted to do, never mind about being a Jew and going to the Brick Lane Talmud Torah. I had heard Caruso, Zenatello, Martinelli, on gramophone records, and I wanted to be like them! I wanted to aim for the highest and the best!

Next I must tell about a three months' holiday I had under the auspices of some Jewish organization which wasn't anything to do with the LCC's Country Holiday Fund for deprived children and its holidays at Leighton Buzzard on the cheap when nobody bothered and all we did was go for walks and maybe once in a while go to the pictures. This holiday was different. I want to quote the name and address of the man who ran it—Mr Greene, Palestine House, Hadleigh, Suffolk. In the three months I stayed in his holiday house in 1934, the year after I went up into the Seniors, I grew up, I changed from a four foot six midget into a five foot seven boy, I put on about three stone in weight, I turned a dark, marvellous brown and I'd never tanned in my life before, and my voice changed from alto to chesty tenor.

Palestine House was a large farmhouse without a farm. Mrs Greene was always ailing but there was also a very willing girl called Marie, about eighteen, with a broad Devon accent and engaged—you know these long engagements in the country; he'd probably be a sailor saving up to earn money, come home and take her away from it all. The house had a profuse garden with apple trees, bushes and a small pool for fishes. Mr Greene used to bury human excrement in it and, after a month when it became dry, we were allowed to dig up our own shit and make little treasure chests and cats and dogs and horses with penknives and pointed bits of wood. There wasn't an indoor lavatory. There was a box-type thing outdoors and you went in, sat on the seat and there was a tin underneath from which Mr Greene drained all the liquid and then put the bowel movements into the ground as fertilizer.

We were about twelve boys and Mr Greene insisted that we write a letter home once a week. We slept in two rooms. The weather was beautiful. One group would help Marie to clean all the utensils and scrub the wooden tables and sweep up. Mr Greene was always improving his garden so there'd also be a few of us who'd go to help build a rockery for a couple of hours. We carried the rocks from nearby ditches. We also helped him build an outhouse for storing coal and vegetables in the winter-time. Later we played in the fields with a bat and a ball and, in the evening, we played card games and guessing the number of peanuts or matchsticks in a hand behind the back, or whether the number was odd or even. Every now and then we were encouraged to entertain one another and, at Mr Greene's request, I used to sing 'Where'er You Walk', 'Where the Bee Sucks' and 'Hark, Hark the Lark'. In the country you have to do the best you can.

But more important than the things we did was the attitude of this man, Mr Greene. When he wanted us to do something, it wasn't, 'You're going to do it because you're living with me, I'm keeping you and I'm feeding you.' No. We were like members of his family. Mr Greene would like a rockery, Mr Greene would like an outhouse, and we'd also enjoy the rockery, we'd also enjoy the outhouse. He was your typical English countryman, slow talking, slow moving, full of humour, always busy in the house or garden. He was about five foot nine or ten, and probably weighed two hundred and forty to two hundred and fifty pounds—very powerful, very good condition. He was almost like a father to us—but not that bully type of father—a good friend and a good companion. One thing I did *not* like about him, though, was the way he insisted on bathing us all once a week on Fridays. His hairy arms used to irritate my skin. And there are two other things which, looking back over the years, I would criticize. We couldn't spend our money as we wanted to. He took it and put it into a common pool and gave us all boiled sweets and chocolates instead, and then, when it was time to go home, if we had any money to our credit, we had to buy boxes of chocolates which he had in stock to take back to our families. The other thing I didn't like was his giving us our best breakfast on the day we left. It was the only day we got bacon and egg, and the bacon was home cured. The idea was that, when a boy got home and his mother and father asked him what he had for food, he'd say, 'Well, for breakfast today we had bacon and egg.' It was psychological.

While I was at Palestine House a big occasion was in the offing. My brother, Morry, was going to get married within a few weeks of my return.

The marriage took place at the Great Garden Street Synagogue. The reception was somewhere in Hackney. Only two things spoiled it. My sister made herself dopey with the wine and just sat there giggling, and the waiters were rushing the courses too fast. We started with an hors d'oeuvre of chopped herring. I think I had half of that when they removed my plate and gave me a bowl of soup. I had two or three spoonfuls of that and they whipped *that* away. Then I got a piece of boiled fish and some chreyn (horseradish and beetroot). They allowed me to partake of two bites, and then away. I then insisted that I have a poulka. By the time I got one good bite out of the meat, away again. I then got a portion of apple strudel which I devoured, being very hungry at the time. After that I had a cup of tea with milk and I listened to the speeches. The rabbi made a big 'un, extolling the marriage and the virtues of both sides of the family, adding the old adage that a marriage begins when you get married and it don't stop, you've got to work at it. Then came the counter-speeches from each of the families who toasted one another, revived old memories of those who were ill, passed over, couldn't make it. There were dozens and dozens of telegrams and good wishes from everybody and anybody.

Then came the moment before the dancing started. The food had been eaten. The speeches had been made. Morry in bobtails, looking very handsome as usual, and his bride, Milly, looking beautiful, as all brides do, in a beaded tiara and white, silken gown, very gingerly took each other in their arms and danced the first dance, 'Unless', beneath a soft, white spotlight—a very touching, poignant memory, with the crowd in a large circle applauding them as they finished the dance.

Unless you give me your sunny smile,
Unless you make living worth the while,
Unless you will be so tender to me,
Then life will be just empty time.

That wedding cost about three pound a couple for fifty couples. We went to the reception on the bus. Alan's wedding in 1946 or '47 for the same numbers cost twenty pound a couple plus another two hundred pound for cars and floral decorations. Alan went up to the rabbi, who was eating and drinking, of course, because a rabbi will grab anything that you haven't got nailed down, and says, 'Give a good droshe (speech)!' and bunged him a fiver. He wasn't to know that the mother-in-law had done the same thing. That man spoke for an hour! People were falling asleep and the youngsters wanted to dance, but he went on and on and on.

1934, the same year as Morry's wedding, I had to start learning my parshah, my bit, my passage from the Sefer Torah for being Bar Mitzvah'd, that is, to become a man who could join a minyon (ten men who make a congregation) and technically bear arms and get married. You have to learn part of the scroll and sing it to a tune which is always the same. If you're lucky and there's nobody with you that's paid, you might get to sing four or five lines. If somebody's with you that's paid, you're lucky to sing one line. Mr French, my teacher at the Talmud Torah, had a Van Dyke beard and a moustache. All he was doing was drumming in my words from the scroll as well as that tune. It got automatic. It was forty years ago. The words I've forgotten but the melody lingers on. I was really concentrating. I thought I was going to do my thing and sing this tune and make everybody happy, including my mother and my brothers and my sister.

The day arrived, Saturday, July the 22nd or 23rd, 1935. The ceremony was at eleven o'clock in the Brick Lane Synagogue, in the same building as the Talmud Torah. A middle-aged man with no voice did two lines of the day's parshah. He'd probably paid two or three pounds. A young boy did one line. Probably cost his father a pound. I hated him. He was better looking than me and dressed smarter. Another man. A couple more boys. All with money. At last it came to my turn. I said a little prayer with my stammer as I was nervous. There was no line left for me to sing. 'Genug, shoyn!' That means 'Enough!' I wasn't paying.

Invited to my Bar Mitzvah party afterwards were over thirty people, including schoolfriends and friends in Carter House. My mother and brothers had all pitched in. We had a table which, when you opened up both sides, was about seven foot long. It and a couple of smaller tables were covered with sandwiches, cakes, tea and lemonade. I was sitting there, at the head of the table, expecting everyone to turn up. But only Sidney Conrich turned up, from next door. His mother—God rest her soul—gave him, for him to give to me, three or four Irish linen handkerchiefs. There's a Jewish festival called the Succoth. In the Jewish Infants' School we had a temple for it covered with leaves, and we were asked if we would contribute say half a pound of sugar or a couple of bananas or an apple, and put them in the temple so they could be given later to the poor. One year me and Betty gave a couple of apples and a couple of bananas, and Mrs Conrich—God rest her soul—came along afterwards and copped her whack because her husband was a presser and on part-time or no-time as days before the war were hard. Now she was returning that favour with the handkerchiefs. When I was Bar Mitzvah'd, Sidney, her son, was the only one to come to the reception. Down he sat, and he and my sister and a couple of brothers and me, we had a little bit of a party. There I was at the head of the table with enough seats for twenty-four to thirty people and a big white table-cloth and enough grub to feed an army—and with only one guest! I don't know to this day why the rest never came. Was it because we had a reputation? Was it because there was always shouting and punching in our flat? It's true that what might be a normal exchange of words between others could be a declaration of war between us. No candlesticks were used, though. It was fists only until my mother hit someone with her broomstick, and that meant the fight was over. But there are certain customs that should be observed. People should have come.

At the top of the Jewish Free School there was a teacher who was a noted poet and a world-wide authority on Charles Lamb. His name was Mr S. M. Rich. Once, when I was in a wrong queue, someone pushed me, and I pushed the boy in front who got nasty. I explained to Mr Rich that I was pushed from behind and he said, 'It's all right.' With Mr Rich I'd have had refinement—music, poetry, painting, carving. Instead I had Pig Isaacs in plus-fours for football and cricket. He had a stammer himself and he hated me. His lessons were 'B-b-b'. He never spoke to me. A man who stammers and is intolerant of other stammerers isn't very nice. My only consolation during that last year was being chosen for the Duke's Place Synagogue Choir and the newly formed Habonim Choir which sang Hebrew and English songs at functions all over London.

It was always my pride as a young boy that the LCC and the Jewish Free School chose July the 21st of each year to terminate for the summer holidays. July the 21st was my birthday. All my school life I knew, come my birthday, that that was the end of schooling until about eight weeks' time. But in July, 1936, when I was fourteen years old, there was no coming back in eight weeks' time. I left school for good. I was shown the door, thrown out. It was, 'Don't come back. We'll get in touch with *you*!'

THREE

Christian firms did not employ Jews. Jews were mostly restricted to the narrow confines of tailoring, cabinet making and street trading. I saw a card in the window of Steele Brothers—WANTED BOY TO LEARN THE TRADE. They made ornamental patterns on mirrors and bevelled the edges before sending them to the silversmith's for coating at the back and framing. I stuck it out for two or three months at the glorious salary of ten bob a week till the boss started asking me to sit in his car minding the stock while he went round doing business. That was in addition to the bevelling. I was never allowed to waste a moment. I asked for an increase. 'No!' I was lucky to be paid at all, apprentices usually paid their guvnors.

So I went up to the Jewish Board of Guardians at the top of Middlesex Street. They gave me an address, a manufacturer of ladies' coats and costumes. But another boy from the Board had applied about an hour before me. The guvnor said, 'I'm giving him a chance.' I went back and told the Board. They said, 'What about Park Royal, the engineers?'

The firm in Park Royal was probably the only Jewish firm in engineering. The two guvnors worked as workers, pretending they were not the guvnors, but they were the guvnors. I was put on the staff with two or three non-Jews doing little jobs for ten bob a week.

At Park Royal we made staircases. We also lacquered objects of pressed brass. Say it was a square pressed in brass of 'Whistler's Mother', it was taken downstairs and sprayed with a lacquer, then, when it had dried out, given a quick polish with a rag. There was also a silver-plating bath where one of the guvnors did the work. He wouldn't let anybody else near it, but me and the lads used to take a penny and dip it in so it came out like a two bob bit. I'd been working there six weeks when I rebelled. When I took the shilling a day fare-money plus the cost of food off my salary, I was losing money, yet the only time the senior partner got sentimental was when he talked about his mother. I walked out. How I envied the kids at my old school only fifty yards from where I lived! There they were without any worries while I was supposed to be working, and I didn't have a job to go to that I liked.

The turning point was at fifteen. I was walking down Greenfield Street and I saw a notice in Mr Hirsh, the tailor's window, No. 9, saying APPRENTICE WANTED. I showed him my School Leavers' Certificate, and he took me on for the usual sum of ten bob a week. That was 1937. He built it up to 37/6d by 1939.

I worked for Mr Hirsh from eight o'clock in the morning till seven o'clock at night, five days a week, and came in on Saturday or Sunday, too, if asked. My first task every morning was to sweep up all the rubbish that had accumulated during the previous day. Then I had to pull the white cotton bastings out of six to eight coats. By now it was probably tea-time. After tea, I basted round the cuffs or pocket flaps with a needle and cotton, or else I put linings onto the sleeves and tacked up the two seams. Come about eleven o'clock and I'd done all the bits and pieces the guvnor asked me to, I'd to carry garments in an all-purpose, very light, canvas sack called 'the wrapper' to one of four shops, including Selfridges. I deposited these on the table where the shop wanted them, put the next batch of garments to be made up in the wrapper and took the bus back again. It was now about half past twelve and I walked home and had my dinner for which I was allowed a full hour. During the afternoon, I soaped and felled collars. In 'soaping' you rub a bar of rough yellow soap, of the kind I was later to use in the army for cleaning floors, to put a bit of body into the material and also to help it stick properly when the presser comes to put it on the iron. Even with cheap rubbish you can create the illusion of a good heavy worsted. 'Felling' is making a shape that will remain by close stitching. I stitched not the material on top but the melton underneath and worked in a little brown canvas so as to give collars a roll. They could then be put onto the garments without any shaping. I made a 'roll' for lapels as well.

At four o'clock I'd have a quick cup of tea, then off I went on a shorter journey than in the morning, delivering and collecting again. When I came back at about half past five, I might pull the bastings out of half a dozen or so coats till seven to keep the presser supplied as he went on till eight. For the same day's work today I'd get not a paltry 37/6d a week but £35 after tax.

I used to think in my ignorance that it was a con game, that we were working at all hours on rubbish and selling it for fancy prices. We were cheap to medium class, yet, by the standards of today, if you put on a suit from us you were wearing a good one. You could even have the button-holes and edges stitched by hand for a couple of shillings extra charge. We hadn't a basting machine, a felling machine, an over-locking machine, a buttoning machine, and so we didn't make mass-produced rubbish.

The staff, apart from me, worked on piece rates—eightpence, tenpence or a shilling a garment. A man who worked hard and didn't go out for lunch could earn five or six pounds a week.

One thing I learned especially. When you're preparing cloth, don't have a cold or eat anything. Cloth absorbs all smells and germs in the vicinity. They are resuscitated by steam or an iron. Your cold will come out again, so will the smell of your pickled cucumber or meat or fried fish.

In 1939 tailoring went out the window. For three months I did nothing. Then I worked for a building firm, mixing cement and carrying bricks and tiles. Then I went on a course in Slough on repairing damaged fuselages and wings of aeroplanes by putting in fresh alloy panels with a rivet-gun.

Near the end of 1940, at the end of the Phoney War, Mr Hirsh called me back again. I went in on the Monday, Tuesday, Wednesday and Thursday. Then the German High Command found out that I was working. They missed the docks, and the first bomb that was dropped on an East End street was dropped that Thursday night on Greenfield Street between the workshop and the house of No. 9, while the Hirsh family were in the basement listening to the wireless. They suffered minor injuries and shock. I never got paid for those four days.

I went into demolition, shovelling the dirt for a firm called Griffiths. At the beginning of 1941 when I was about eighteen and a half, I received a notice from the War Office saying I was to report for a medical examination to the Territorial Drill Hall at Whipps Cross which was a recruiting centre for all three services. I bent down. They looked up to see whether the hat was on straight, and they told me I was A1. I asked could I join the RAF as a ground fitter as I'd been on the course in Slough. No. No more needed. The navy was scrubbed out right away because I was Jewish and the navy was the last bastion of polite anti-Semitism. 'It's the Infantry for you. You're a fit boy.' I remember buying a second-hand record of Caruso singing 'O Paradiso' and 'On with the Motley' when I got outside. Then at the age of nineteen and a half, in the last week of December, 1941, I got the shock of my life. I received a greeting card from the King, opened it up and read, 'Welcome to the British Army'. Enclosed was a four bob Postal Order, two days' pay, and I was to report to the Second Battalion of the Royal Ulster Rifles in Aylesbury.

Talking about the war, at the time of the Declaration, the London groups of the Habonim had a last meeting at Woburn House, Red Lion Square. About five hundred of us were present, including Olga Braham and Lily Barak, head women in the organization, who asked us to keep in touch by writing to them at headquarters even if we were called up or evacuated. At the end of the meeting, one of them told us that boys and girls were needed on the David Eder Farm in Maidstone to clear the weeds which were growing six feet high and choking the mangel-wurzels. The job had to be done within two or three weeks, otherwise the crops could be written off and the cows would die of hunger as there was feed as well as food rationing. Along with some college students and grammar schoolboys I volunteered. Eder Farm, before the war, was run by Zionists to train Jewish men and women in farming before they went to Israel. Even the cows there were called by Hebrew names. In the two or three years before the outbreak of war, many German and Austrian Jewish refugees came to England and went to work on the farm, firstly because they couldn't get any other job and secondly because they wanted to go to Israel. At the beginning of the war, the refugees, who represented two-thirds of the working force of sixty, were detained, leaving the farm undermanned. Hence the present crisis and the need to save the winter crop.

I remember working over the fields in the sunshine to save that crop. After our stay there, walking back to the station along a dirt track sloping gently downwards, we saw a German fighter being chased by a Spitfire in the blue sky above us. We could hear the Spitfire's guns flashing da-da-da-boom-boom as it passed. Then, a few miles in the distance, we saw the German plane go into a slow half-dive and then there was a whoom of smoke rising from some trees. Some of the youngsters cheered. For them it was like a scene out of a film. But this was no film. On the train I said to myself, 'By God! No parachute! The pilot couldn't have got out!'

To get back to the dedicated passion which I haven't talked about for far too long! As I said before, I became a young tenor in the Duke's Place Synagogue Choir while I was at the Jewish Free. Manny Fisher and his younger brother, Monty, were tenors in the choir as well. Monty sometimes sang solo with the chazzen. If not him, it was Manny. One day—I was about twelve and a half—someone said to me, 'Monty has a touch of the laryngitis. Why not ask Mr Shute (the choirmaster) if you can sing with the chazzen this week in his place? You've got a big enough voice.' Being young and naïve and ambitious and stupid, I went and quietly spoke to Mr Shute. He said, 'Who do you think you are?!! A pipsqueak who's been here six months wants to sing with the chazzen!!' I said, 'What else?!' He said, 'Do me a favour! Get back in the choir!' I said, 'Stick the choir!' and left.

No more choirs. No more Mulberry Street Choir. No more Habonim Choir. No more Duke's Place Choir. I said to myself, 'There's something better for me. I don't want to sing in harmony any more. My voice is growing. I want to hear it solo singing, no opposition. I don't feel comfortable with all those small voices. I'm having to curb myself. I want to be a choir on my own. I never get any inspiration from Hebraic songs. I may have been born a Jew but I want to be a citizen of the world!' Then I had my sabbatical, as they say, to think things over. And I stuck to my decision, a decision I've never regretted. As the years went by, in my pursuit of perfection, I achieved a standard so high that, with any luck or if this country had been Italy or America, I could have reached the top.

At the age of sixteen and a half, in the September of 1938, I decided it was time I had some proper singing lessons. I went to Toynbee Hall and joined a singing class there which cost 17/6d for a year. By then I was earning about 27/6d a week with Mr Hirsh so I could afford it. I was putting away about three half crowns a week in the Post Office, giving my mother fifteen bob and, with the dollar I had left over, going to the cinema and buying bars of chocolate and the best pipe tobacco, Balkan Sobranie.

Toynbee Hall was named in honour of Arnold Toynbee who went to university and took pity on the poor working-classes of the East End who didn't have much education or appreciation of the Arts. I fitted in there like a very happy bug in a well-known and well-loved rug. It was a realization of all my dreams. From the outside, the buildings weren't particularly impressive. But inside there was an air of drama, beauty, activity, camaraderie. Brilliantly gifted people of the many shades of Art were there—ballet dancers, actors, musicians, singers, painters, sculptors. I stayed there from the end of 1938, when the war was imminent, right on through '39 and '40 to the end of '41. Maybe the war as regards the bombing hadn't hit us very hard at that time, but the Depression which is the earmark of a war was upon the face of the land—except at the Toynbee. The Toynbee never went down. It wasn't even because the people there were young. There were many youngsters like myself, but many others were in their thirties and forties. It was a common meeting-ground of people who had some artistic bent. One person gave forth to another, and the other received it and gave out something of his own to others. The atmosphere was truly magical. It hit me then and, even now as I look back, I still think, 'That was the first time in my life I felt I was really where I belonged'. I was surrounded by people who were like myself. They were searching, they were participating. In an atmosphere almost of gaiety people were talking about their art and their pleasure and their activities. Though in later life I was to join similar institutions, there was a different atmosphere at the Toynbee, a discipline, a tradition, a way of going about things, that inspired confidence. It wasn't a wishy-washy, do-as-you-like organization. There was a canteen where you could meet other people, but when you went into class it was for business, it was for work.

Singing classes were given five days a week by Robert Kent Parker, who was in his early sixties and a glutton for work and money. He was a Canadian, about six foot tall and slim, with a mane of whitey-greyey hair. He went to New York as a young man, was taught by an Italian teacher, and ended with the Manhattan Opera Company singing Wagner in English! His classes began at six o'clock and ran on, with one break in the middle, till nine. I bowled along between half past six and seven every Friday after I'd finished work and had something to eat, and stayed till the end. I planned it that way because, if I'd come along early, he might have been tempted, if he didn't have too many people in front, to make me sing before I had time to digest my meal. I used to sing my song at about half past eight, quarter to nine. The first time I sang, the voice was rather in the head, but it was round and sweet, even if I say so myself. You were only given the one song, and you'd be lucky if he let you sing it all. You might get jammed after the first four lines due to lack of phrasing or feeling or interpretation. The more talent you showed, the harder he became. The mediocres he let sing the whole song. 'Very nice. Thank you.' No criticism. He was a man of finer feelings. He would not tolerate even a hint of a smile when a nervous beginner, or a person of no talent but only the wish to learn, was committing every mistake possible. Some people learn when they hear great voices and somebody explains how they achieve their effects, but I found out, within the first moments of joining that class, that I learned more about the pitfalls an untrained singer has in his path, such as bad breathing, bad phrasing and picking songs beyond his vocal range, than I would if I'd have heard the most perfect voices that God ever gave Man. I was very ambitious and I was right to be so, for a tenor-to-be should recognize no limitations. Even at the age of seventeen, I wanted to sing 'Che gelida manina' ('Your tiny hand is frozen') with the original top C instead of the optional A. Robert Kent Parker said, 'You're young as a singer and, as a tenor, you're very young. Don't try the C yet till it becomes part of your register and you can depend on it.'

One evening I came early, about six. He called me into a room at the back of the hall where he taught us and said my stammering might get better if I were to read aloud. He had spotted my impediment a few weeks before, because Leon Leon, a fireman and a tenor of sorts, had tried to sing 'The Flower Song' from *Carmen* and, in the discussion which followed, I had said rather haltingly, 'You sing it very, very well, Leon, but why make it so dramatic when it's supposed to be a reminiscent love-song?' I never stammered when I sang. Mr Parker said, 'I've told you how my singing teacher in America used to tell me to "Yawn! Yawn! Relax the throat!" Maybe you should relax the throat when you're speaking.'

It didn't help, but I was so spurred by a professional man taking such an interest in me that, within the first three months of joining his class, I sang 'Ay-Ay-Ay' by Freire. The last line of the song was 'And the rose sadly fades before you'. The first time I sang it in public—at an end-of-term concert—I couldn't remember that last line. There was a split second's delay. Mr Parker said to me afterwards, 'Why did you shut your eyes? Was it pain or ecstasy?' I said, 'I forgot the last line!' He said, 'If you forget any words in future just mumble them.'

Miguel Fleta created a sensation with 'Ay-Ay-Ay' in the 1920's. I've heard the record and, frankly, I wouldn't do it the way he did. He used to sing a note and then die it away, shaking it. I fade it away by diaphragm control. I sang that song at three end-of-term concerts, always in front of two to three hundred people. The third time was the best. Mr Mallon, a dear, dear man and Warden of Toynbee Hall, came and congratulated me afterwards. I had given it the same weight all the way through and done the diminuendo at the end properly. The performance was well rounded. I had practised my art.

I had a great respect for Robert Kent Parker. I always called him 'Mr' and I very rarely call anybody 'Mr'. But there were two things for which I've never forgiven him. I was a squat, powerful boy and I looked a bit older than I was, especially as I didn't shave much and had a bit of a beard always come Friday. His son was an officer in the Tank Corps and went missing in the Middle East. Though Mr Parker had my age in his Register and should have known I wasn't due to be called up for another year, he took it out on me by saying, 'Why aren't you in the army?' Then, when I had my call-up papers and I'd only a few months to go, he put forward a soprano, a baritone and a contralto for scholarships to a man from the Royal Academy of Music. I was surprised that he didn't include me, though I was probably the best singer there. The test was this: the man from the Royal Academy struck a note on the piano and you sang it; then you had to mentally think of four notes higher and sing that. That was all the test was! And for that the scholars were to be given free music and free teaching! I waited until the man went, and then I said, 'Pardon me, Mr Parker. You picked out some of the outstanding singers in the class, but I don't think *I*'m one of the worst. Why didn't you let *me* try?' He said, 'Ah, but you're going to be called up in a couple of months, aren't you?' I bore him a grudge for that. Maybe he was a latent anti-Semite. He told us once that Richard Tauber had cut him out of a film of *Pagliacci*.

Nevertheless, his classes were a lot of fun. I remember, above all, doing the quartet from *Rigoletto* with two tenors (me and Leon) and two contraltos on one side of the room, and two baritones and two sopranos on the other. We rehearsed for six weeks. I did the tenor part alone one night when Leon was away. The bit I took most pride in was the phrase 'unrequited love' with which Caruso had to struggle on the B flat at the end of the run. Not me! What a pity we never performed that quartet in the concert at the end of my last term.

He once invited us to bring up some of our favourite gramophone records one Sunday afternoon. I brought along a couple of Caruso records and he said, 'That's not the Caruso that *I* heard!' Apparently Caruso was always recorded for HMV at the speed of 78. But in the very early recordings in 1901-2-3 he sang at the speed of about 81, 82. When you played those records at the speed of 78, the voice went browny and chesty.

Mr Parker was a bass, and unfortunately a bass can't show a tenor how to get his top notes. He showed me the way that you pitch the voice to the back of the head so that it will rebound into the front mask, but he didn't tell me how, when you go over a certain note, you must aim for the *crown* of the head. I learned that by accident at the age of twenty-eight. Before then, my top notes were chesty. From then on, I developed the head tone. But, in spite of the fact he seemed to prefer non-Jewish singers, he gave me a lot of good advice, and I think if I'd been a bit older and a bit less sensitive not only as a Jew but as a singer, because I was always deadly serious, he would have been to me, not only in the off-moments, a very charming, friendly person. It's due to him that my voice, at the age of fifty-one, is still in good trim though it has been in constant use over many years. As he used to say, 'The voice is ninety-five per cent hard work and tricks.' Certain rules I learned at the Toynbee I agreed with and kept to. There is a tradition, there is a history, there is a continuation of style and standards of singing which he was able to impart.

Though from recordings and broadcasts *I* considered that the late twenties and the early thirties was the period of the really great tenors—Gigli, Martinelli, Zenatello, Lauri-Volpi—*he* preferred to talk about the golden singers of the early 1900's, such stars, for instance, as Nellie Melba, Tudor Davies and Jean de Reske. He once appeared in a charity show with Caruso. He said that, when Caruso sang 'M'appari tutt'amor' with his foot on a stool, he felt sick with envy because Caruso sang so easy. I've got news for Mr Parker. I could sit in the bath, open my bowels, eat a four course dinner, and *still* sing 'M'appari tutt'amor'! It's *easy* for a tenor! Caruso had no more than a lovely lyrical voice with a limited range which he never abused. He was no heldentenor.

The best advice Mr Parker ever gave me was when I was trying during my second year to sing 'Your tiny hand is frozen'. I couldn't get that line right which finished with a top C and has an A before it, so he took me to the wall and made me stand with my back to it about six inches away. 'Now,' he said, 'when you take the end of that line, I'm going to push you, and I want you to fall back against the wall but to keep singing.' Out came a beautiful top C! He was showing that, with the aid of the diaphragm, I could do it. You can't keep the diaphragm tense all the time. It sometimes needs a kick, so you pick your chest up and tense the diaphragm muscles. I sing, therefore, with my arms half up across the stomach and my shoulders back, leaving the chest free play and room to move the diaphragm. When you hold your hands together or, like some women do, half clasped, you are giving the diaphragm a signal—'Tense up! I'm going out for a top note or I'm going to do a run'. I sing like a fighter. I sing with my feet. Sometimes I grip with them; sometimes I go up on my toes and I bounce—all to give me the drive. If you could see the diaphragm through your stomach, it would look like a plate that's been turned upside down. It's a ridge of muscle just over the stomach. By exerting force to push out your lower rib-box, you push down on the diaphragm which flattens out a bit and you can hold your rib-box in position for as long as you like. This is impossible when you've just eaten. So, when you're going to open up and sing big, when you're going to stand up and deliver, when you're going to go into super-drive, never do so on a full stomach. You'll be playing too much on the throat, and what is the throat but two thin tissues of skin which vibrate. It won't be able to take the strain.

Mr Parker probably only gave me four or five other good tips altogether. He told me how to use the silent H to help with top notes. If you've got a word like 'love' on a top note, you sing 'lo-hove'. You're not sounding the H but you're using extra force, you're putting a bit more effort into the diaphragm and the tone comes out fuller because you've opened up your throat and mouth. Same with the word 'because'. 'Bec-hause'. You get a certain push and power in the middle of the word. Someone once said about someone's performance at a Toynbee concert it was a pity that his silent H's weren't so silent. Mr Parker certainly set me on the road to thinking of the best and easiest way to achieve an effect. 'If you sing a good note,' he said, 'stand in front of the mirror to see the shape of your mouth.' I found from that that I got a better tone when I was half smiling. He said, 'Look above the heads of your audience. Regard them as a row of cabbages. In that way they won't put you off.' In time I learned to look so near to the crown of their heads that they thought I was looking at *them* but I wasn't. Another tip was that you sing on the breath and not with the breath, another that amplification comes from the acoustic chambers of the chest for the low notes and the head bones for the high. As regards interpretation he said, 'Don't just sing a song anyhow. Read the lyric, see what it means, then work out your build-up, vary your approach to make the song interesting.' Maybe listening to the chazzens in the Synagogue when I was a young boy taught me more than Mr Parker on this point, because a chazzen will never sing the same way all the time, he'll use many shades of power and colour during the one religious song. The chazzens taught me how to keep an audience alive. It didn't know what I was going to do until I did it.

Lying in bed at No. 18, Carter House or sitting in the loo or standing in our main room for one or two hours a day from Monday to Friday, I softly practised scales and runs and songs, and, at the week-ends when I was on my own, I used to give the voice an airing for three or four hours. Quite apart from the repertoire of Irish and Neapolitan songs and Schubert lieder I built up at home, I must have worked on a dozen songs in my three years at the Toynbee, including 'Ay-Ay-Ay', 'Because', 'Trees', 'For You Alone', 'Your tiny hand is frozen', 'On with the Motley', 'The Flower Song'. Tosti's 'Parted' had a deeper meaning for me than just the words:

Dearest, our day is over
Ended the dream divine
You must go back to your life
I must go back to mine
Back to the joyless duties
Back to the fruitless tears
Loving and yet divided
All through the empty years.
How could I live without you
How could I let you go
I that you love so well, dear
You that I worship so
You that I worship so—

I wasn't simulating the emotions when I sang that song. I was thinking of a girl called Nettie. But that's another story.

I was now a lirico spinto, a full-blooded tenor with a lyrical line. I could sing robust, or soft and sweet. My range was unlimited. I could sing two octaves above middle C and two octaves below middle C, and the normal range of a singer in opera is only about two octaves, there's no call for any more. And what I had to do was go into the army!!

FOUR

A blind, unreasoning hatred of people or a colour is hard to understand. I've been in lodgings at the 46, Cavell Street for six years where I used to think we were a very cosmopolitan, very enlightened community that got along. Apart from the landlord who's Maltese, there are sixteen of us—there's four or five Irish (mostly Southern), a Welshman, a Chinaman, three Jews and, here and there, some Englishmen. We've had a few whores and married couples stay for a while, but it's predominantly a male chauvinistic preserve. The Welshman has now joined the Irish in getting drunk, and his version of two hundred and twenty-six choruses of 'I'll Take You Home Again Kathleen' at two o'clock in the morning is a classical piece of consistently tuneless stamina. I once pointed out that two hundred and twenty-six choruses of the same song was a bit too much, but he took it in good part at the time. In fact, I almost got along with everybody. They were working people. There was an air of camaraderie through the power cuts and so on. They called me 'the man with the candle'—a bit of friendly sniping, but nothing insulting. To me, religion, race and colour mean nothing. I treat people as I want to be treated myself. Six years we've lived in happiness and harmony, but now, due to propaganda in the papers, the Jews have become the villains again and the drunken Irish bums have got mixed up in their thinking. There's an Irishman in the building trade. When he's drunk he says, 'Hi, Jew boy!' It's not a greeting like, 'Howya, Joe!' or 'Howya, Harry!' It's aggressive and insulting. I once told him, I said, 'John, you know my name like I know your name. I don't say, "Hi, you Roman Catholic asterisk asterisk!" Call me by my name, Alex, like I call you John!' He took no notice. Maybe I should belt him one. When I was twelve, there was a boy I belted called Billy Wall—a redhead and a Roman Catholic who insulted me for being Jewish. His sister started it. She said, 'If you beat that Jew I'll get you confirmed.' I found I was the greatest fighting champion of the world. I fought like Ted Kid Lewis. I powdered him. I clouted him in the guts and head. I bounced him off the deck so many times he got tired of getting up.

You'll always find a minority who are prejudiced, whether it's against the Jews, the Americans or the Negroes. Every country's got them. They're pigs. And in the army I met so many pigs, so many anti-Semites, that in the end I had to ask to be released.

When I reported to the 2nd Battalion of the Royal Ulster Rifles in Aylesbury during the first week of January, 1942, it was so bitterly cold and there was so much snow and ice that I couldn't wait to get into my uniform. We settled down to six months' marching and PT and being taught how to use the anti-tank rifle, the Lee Enfield rifle, the bren gun, the tommy gun, the .45 revolver, the two inch and the four inch mortar and the hand grenade. My number was 7022437. I remember it because I'd to duplicate it with a stencil on every article of clothing they gave me.

I was probably the only soldier not a bandsman who went to war carrying his music—forty to fifty songs, mostly operatic arias and Victorian ballads. I kept them between two pieces of hardboard joined together with canvas like a book, and tied around. I'd only been in Aylesbury about a week when, queuing up in the canteen for a cup of tea and a wad, I heard Menuhin playing Mendelssohn's Violin Concerto on the wireless. I started crying. A couple of rookies asked me why. I said, 'Listen to that beautiful music! I'm homesick!' Half a dozen or so started to laugh. Mind you, some of them were cowards and cried only in the night-time.

That same week, the colonel, Lt Col Cairn, arranged a concert by members of the battalion to welcome the new recruits. He concluded the programme himself by singing 'A bachelor gay am I' and then announced that he would welcome a return concert by the new recruits themselves. Plans were made. A lieutenant who was a good pianist organized a cast—myself, himself, a couple of jugglers, a couple of would-be comedians, an impressionist and a singer of popular songs. Two or three rehearsals were called, then the lieutenant went on leave and we never saw him again. No concert. It was one of the mysteries of life.

Music or no music, I soon acquired a bit of a reputation as a boxer, sparring with Jack Darling, a London boy and a beautiful boxer who would have been a World Champion if he'd survived the war. I was a middle-weight. The first time I saw him I thought, 'By God, he's six foot and he must weigh about fourteen stone!' Then I saw him stripped. He was a welter-weight, slim on the hip and also on the leg, though I've never seen a broader pair of shoulders in my life. His arms, though they weren't too heavy, were well muscled and carried a dig. He wasn't a Jew but, Jew or Gentile, he didn't care.

Jack first saw me in the gymnasium in front of the big, heavy punchbag. I was throwing short ones and the bag was really moving. I'd just had a few collisions in a hand-ball game with a Welshman who'd been a boxing champion before the war, and the PTI had said, 'You'll sort it out at half five in the gymnasium.' Jack agreed to be my second. He advised me to get close, keep close and hook it to the body because the other had the reach. During the fight I was hitting this Welshman round the body and it flashed through my mind how Bob FitzSimmons had put paid to Gentleman Jim Corbett in the World Heavyweight Title fight after his wife, Rosie, shouted, 'Hit him in the slats!', which means the Derby Kelly, the belly, and he used the solar plexus punch. I did the same. I swivelled on my hip. I kept my elbow next to my side and I hit him the short one. It was devastating. My fist didn't move more than six inches. His breath left his body in a gush. He just went Boom! His face turned green and he went out like a kipper gasping for breath and had to be given artificial respiration.

At the time of the Coming Out Parade after the first six weeks of heavy training, everyone in our hut pitched in about half a quid for a celebration in the boozer in Stone Village near a side-gate of the Castle. I only had a beer and a couple of whisky chasers, and I'd packed in a good meal first. The rest got pie-eyed, so they asked me to lead them back past the guard just before twelve. About forty of us formed a long chain, and I was at the head of the conga which was supposed to be a march. Half fell into the ditches on the side of the road and, when at last we got through the gate, you've never seen such zig-zagging and ins and outs of the slit trenches as the conga line continued its way to our hut!

It was time for my first leave, and this is where I can tell why I found special meaning in the words of Tosti's 'Parted'.

When I was eleven, twelve, thirteen, and still with the Joseph Trumpeldor group of the Habonim, there was another group, the Gedud Naomi group, the female version, which used to come along on the Monday or Tuesday. One girl—ooh she was nice! She had bluey-green eyes, red hair, freckles and a lovely smile. She was tall, slim and warm-natured. Her name was Nettie. A group of us—a couple of girls and a couple of fellows—were always listening to records, or concerts on the wireless, at her house. I used to sing 'The stars are brightly shining' from *Tosca* for her, also 'The strange harmony of love' from the same opera. I very much liked her. She was going to Raine's. She was a natural lady, she didn't have to put on airs. Her father was a wholesaler with dresses, costumes and coats on display in a showroom in the New Road, so her parents weren't poor. They had good food and there was a good table-cloth and they wore nice clothes. For the East End they were 'all right'. For five or six years Nettie accepted me as a friend. She ignored the difference in our station. We held hands. We walked arm in arm. She made me feel so comfortable that, with her, I never stammered. If I'd had any prospects in some sort of a business or as a singer, I'd have declared my true feelings.

Two things happened to settle the matter. Firstly, when I was just over nineteen, I was called up, and secondly, while I was away, her parents introduced her to a tall, blond, good-looking, intelligent captain in the Medical Corps to enable her to avoid going into the forces. I met him when I came home on leave and went to see her. I said to myself, 'Look, Alex, you must come out and tell the girl that you care for her very much, and would she consider seeing you on future leaves and, please God, if things work out, you'll do something worthwhile for the future.'

She's not in when I get there. Her mother says, 'Oh, Nettie's engaged! She's engaged to a captain in the Medical Corps!' What could I do? Burst into tears? Within about five minutes, as if it had been rehearsed, Nettie comes in with this tall, big captain. 'How are you getting on, Nettie? I'm very pleased to hear about your engagement.' That's the only thing I *could* say! What else could I do but offer her my congratulations?

They were married, and I used to see her occasionally after the war. She looked faded. She had lost her sparkle. I said to her once, 'Don't let this affect your feelings or your thoughts too much, but I really did care for you when we were younger, and I still care for you.' 'Why didn't you tell me?!' she said. 'Because I didn't have anything to give you or to offer,' I replied. A pause off-stage for inward sobs!

I returned to the Royal Ulsters when my leave in 1942 was over. It had some really nice, friendly boys. But there's always a fly or two in the ointment. An anti-Semitic sod of a sergeant decided to persecute me during the Tiger Stunt, an exercise in invading tactics for the entire Division under Montgomery before he assumed command of the 8th Army in the Middle East. Our brigade consisted of the Royal Ulster Rifles, 2nd Battalion, the Queen's Own Scottish Borderers and the Welsh mob, the Buffs. Every hour you had to change over weapons. You could be carrying the anti-tank rifle which, with the ammunition, weighed sixty or seventy pounds and, after that, have to carry a bren gun or a tommy gun. But *I* was carrying the anti-tank rifle for three hours at a time, and it was by sheer accident that I got changed. Then, when we got to a rest in the early mornings, somehow I was always given the first of the sentry-goes, and somehow I'd to be on sentry-go for three or four hours, and nobody told me I should take off my boots so my feet swelled up like bloaters.

The stunt finished off on the night of the ninth day. We were picked up in the TCL's (troop-carrying lorries) and driven somewhere with Nissen huts where the whole brigade was supposed to stay till the individual TCL's picked us up and took us back to our own battalions. It was nine or ten o'clock. I was dead tired. I'd lost ten to twelve pounds in weight. I'd had very little sleep. The sort of bloody stupid thing they'd pretended were that our blankets couldn't arrive because they'd been knocked out by enemy action, and that the food supply truck had been bombed—so I'd had very little grub and very little sleep, either. Come that night, I was so tired and so slow I couldn't get on to one of the bunks, I just lay down on the floor exhausted. All of a sudden I heard a sergeant's voice shouting, 'Keep on! Keep on! Keep on!' I was saying in my mind, 'I can't keep on! I'm tired! I'm tired!' *Still* he shouted, 'Keep on! Keep on!' I opened my eyes and found it had been a nightmare and that I'd crawled the entire length of the hut!

We had seven or eight hours' kip and got back to base after about two hours swaying and bobbing on a truck. The colonel said, 'Dismissed!', we saluted and broke off to make our way to our huts. But this dirty bastard of a sergeant—and it was like the nightmare—said, 'Go on, Hartog! Hurry up! Get to your hut! Get to your hut!' I said, 'I'm *going*!' 'Don't argue with me! Get to your hut!' I said, 'I'm *going*!' He said, 'You're on a charge of insubordination!'—and, what's more, he made it stick. I still feel bad about that fucking bastard.

At least in the Guard House I had the first night's sleep I'd had in a long time. Next morning I came in front of the colonel. The sergeant told lies. He said I refused to obey orders and was truculent and showed dumb insolence. I explained the circumstances as clearly as I could, though I was keyed up and my impediment was hindering me. I said I was tired at the time; I hadn't had much sleep on the stunt; I'd had very little food; I was always being put on sentry-go; my feet were swollen and I'd even got swollen knees. What was the rush? Did I have to drop down dead because the sergeant insisted I gallop off the Parade Ground?

I thought I'd convinced the colonel. He said, to me, 'Will you accept the punishment?' I said, 'Yes.' I didn't, like a good Yiddisher boy, say, 'Yes, if you tell me what the punishment is and I deserve it.' I got twenty-eight days' field punishment, the largest amount of punishment you could have without leaving the Battalion and going to Colchester where you did everything on the double with a rifle over your head or wearing a full pack.

So I'd to answer every bugle-call—reveille, meal-time, letter-time . . . There were eight to ten of them, and I'd to be there. It didn't matter what I was doing, I'd to drop everything and report at the Guard House flag in full kit for inspection. Then there were the tins. I was given a tin and some sand and some water and I had to scrape the tin clean. That took a couple of hours until they slung it away and you got the next dirty one.

On completion of my bird, I asked the CSM could I see Captain Hyde, the Company Commander. I marched on my own in full dress uniform to the A Company hut and I spoke to Captain Hyde. I told him straight, 'I don't like your stinking battalion! I want a transfer! When I could do the whole of that stunt and finish up exhausted and then be put on a charge and framed for twenty-eight days' punishment! I want a transfer and I don't care where!' He said, 'Well, there's only one way you'll go, and that's down!' I said, 'Send me where you like!' So ended my nine or ten months in the Royal Ulster Rifles. So began my saga of see the rest of the British Army in a hurry, hang on to your haversack and away we go.

The day I was transferred I didn't say anything but it was in my mind that, if I met that bastard sergeant who framed me, I'd boot his bollocks off. But the word had already spread. The boys made up his bed so it collapsed. Someone slapped a big pile of water over him. He tripped over a wire. He was given about ten hidings. I believe he eventually asked for a transfer and they slung him out of the mob without a stripe.

Next stop two months. My music safely at the back of my haversack, I was transferred to the Pioneer Corps at Mary Hill Barracks, Glasgow, the No. 1 Food Supply Depot for the United Kingdom. Among the bays you felt you were in enormous canyons. Our job was to unload food-boxes of tinned milk, sugar, Maconachy stew, cigarettes, boiled sweets, bars of chocolate—enough for an emergency meal for one day for twelve men—off the train trucks and load them onto lorries to be taken to the warehouses or the ships.

The day I arrived I went to the canteen after settling in and was in time to see the second half of a concert put on by two ladies of the district—a leading Scottish soprano and her accompanist. After singing her last song—something from *Bitter Sweet*—and complaining that the ceiling was too low, she invited members of the audience to come up and entertain. After two or three so-called singers had done their stuff, I stood up and asked if they had the music of any songs good for a tenor voice. She said, 'Yes,' and I sang 'Down in the Glen' and 'Bonny Mary from Argyll'. The pianist and the singer were smiling because they recognized one of their own. No one would step up after me. I spoke to the two ladies about where I came from and where I learned my technique, then I stepped down and went to have a cup of tea. On my way to the counter I overheard a couple of our cockney intellectuals say to one another, 'Where did *that* flash git come from?' It put me right off singing for *them*.

A week or two afterwards when I was working in the bays I heard a young soldier who fancied himself as a tenor. An Anglo-Italian corporal was in charge of us. He saw me with a wry smile on my face and said, 'Have *you* done some singing?' I said, 'Some!' He said, 'We've nothing to do for the next quarter of an hour. How about obliging?' I obliged with 'For You Alone' and some numbers from *The Student Prince*. The power of my voice filled the bays. My top notes were bouncing off the ceilings. Unlike my audience in the canteen who weren't impressed, the good two hundred men working in the bays *were*, and showed their appreciation with tumultuous applause. I'm sorry to say the young tenor who fancied himself as a tenor never sang again. Pity.

At Mary Hill Barracks I seemed to come up against all the rough and scruffs and slags of Great Britain, with their hatreds and their pre-formed conceptions. There was a Welshman from the Rhondda Valley who thought that, because I was a Jew, I should have had horns. He gave me a horrified look. He said, 'You're a *Jew*?!!'

One Sunday afternoon, it was raining. No one could go anywhere till six. About forty of us were sitting around in the hut talking, including the corporal, who was supposed to be a Scottish 'honourable'. Now you could see that thirty-five of them were very nice. Doesn't matter where from. Nice people. But there were two bastards—one from the back doubles of Bermondsey and the other from Birmingham. Three others are their hangers-on and join in with them and laugh—snide, ha!

ha! I was an arguer then with the facts and figures as I am now. As the questions come, I answer. The Bermondsey boy brought up how, when you were walking along Whitechapel Road or the Commercial Road, all you could see was foreign Jewish names. I said, 'Course you see Jewish names in a Jewish area where Jewish people are giving work to the rest! What names do you expect? Irish and Welsh? They're not going to change their names for you or anybody!' . . . I got a bit heated. Everybody started talking about whether Hitler was right or not. I said, 'If you don't win this bleeding war you'll find out he was wrong!' It ended up that, though I was giving clear answers that even an idiot could understand, nobody seemed to be on my side, not even the Scottish 'honourable'. I'm at my best when under fire. 'Should Britain be in the war?' To that I said, 'Hitler has ambitions to conquer the world. He's using the Jew as a scapegoat to get into power, to keep in power and to extend that power. Persecution of the Jews can very soon lead to persecution of others. Just let him get to this country, and you'll see how he'll discriminate, how he'll destroy and imprison the strong ones, the defiant ones, the people who don't think like the normal sheep!'

I was watching the faces, and listening for the sounds of the people who hadn't the brains to hide their feelings, though the ones a Jew is really afraid of are the ones who smile at him and don't show their hatred and he can't guard. I soon pin-pointed the villains—the two I've mentioned, the boy from Bermondsey and the boy from Birmingham.

They were always together. The Bermondsey boy fancied himself as a boxer. He was about my size. He was a middle-weight. I was a bit heavier than a middle-weight, but I used to fight as a middle-weight. The Birmingham boy was a bit shorter than me and squat. I decided to take them on at night-time. There was a fish shop on the very outskirts of Glasgow. From there you had a two-mile hike back to barracks, beginning with a hill. It was dark, no lights. The two of them were tipsy. The Birmingham boy had to relieve himself. He tottered off. That left the Bermondsey boy on his own. I'd been following them twenty or thirty yards behind, keeping to the grass verge. The Bermondsey boy was waiting, eating his fishcake and chips.

I knee-ed him in the crutch and, when he fell, I booted him in the head till he was down and out. It may seem brutal, but it was a culmination. His friend came back and I sent him down on the deck with a good right-hander. I put the boot a few times in *his* head, too, and then I walked off. I'd too many brains to be a Pioneer. They were still away in hospital when I was re-graded and given a transfer as a sapper to the 5th Trainee Battalion of the Royal Engineers in Chester.

Three months' more violence! There was a boy in my hut—I think his name was Cohen. Before the war he'd been an apprentice printer. Do you know the cartoons that the Nazis used to issue, with the black, curly head and the big, hooked nose and the sallow complexion? Well, apart from the fact that he carried sixteen and a half stone of flab, he was a living likeness of the caricature depicted by those cartoons—and he was a coward to boot. There was mickey-taking something lovely. Sometimes it hinted at violence, but there were too many others there for anyone to actually pull a stroke.

The bunks were two-tier. I took a lower one right away. I always felt comfortable low to the ground. A young English boy was over me. Nice fellow. We got along very well. Cohen was on the other side of the hut. One night, the lads were ribbing him, pulling him out of bed with his blankets and his mattress so the poor sod had to make up his bed again in the darkness. It had happened a couple of times. I had a little debate with myself, 'Shall I or shan't I?' We were the only Jews in the hut. They knew *he* was a Jew—me, not yet.

I made my first declaration one day when we were watching how to make a mine safe. There was a drop of about six or seven feet down a slope to a pit where a sergeant was giving a demonstration. Well, I'm about three or four feet back—I never stand on no edge. Four or five of the boys are with this Cohen. They're crowding. Somehow it's a crowded place. They're crowding him closer and closer and closer to that edge. All of a sudden I call out, 'Cohen, come here! There's a bit more room here.' One of the boys says, 'It's all right. He's safe with us.' I say, 'Mind your own effing business! When I tell him to come, I want him to come! I'm talking to *him*!' He came. He realized that he'd found a friend of sorts. I said, 'What are you taking this shit for?! You're a Yiddisher boy! Either you make it or they'll hound you and kill you!' He said, 'I've never been in no fight!' I said, 'Well, start thinking about it!'

We get back to the hut. Cohen and the nice English fellow change bunks. I've said I want to be under Cohen to give him advice on how to clean his rifle—the usual thing that an experienced soldier does. Come the night-time, and the others start. That's when I move out swinging. I've a helmet in one hand, and the other hand made into a fist. I knock two men down, and another one is calling out about what I've done to his nose. All of a sudden the light comes on. Who's looking at the scene? The corporal. 'What's going on here?!' 'Since when,' I said, 'has a British soldier not been allowed to lie in his bunk without a lot of bloody people coming in, attacking him? Don't you know the villains here wait till a person gets into his bed, and then they drag him out and kick him by accident in the dark?! What are we?! Are we in the British Army or the German Army?!' I told him straight. I knew that he knew for about two weeks that this new intake had been suffering night after night. He said to me, 'It's the first time I've heard this noise!' I said, 'It's the first time someone's had the nerve to tell these fucking bastards to keep away from the bunk!' Give that corporal his due, I wasn't charged, and Cohen was never attacked again.

I'd been with the 5th TBRE's about a month, and in the army for sixteen, when I applied to the Company Commander for leave. He said, 'You've officially got another two months to do. If you take your ten days now it means that, when you come back, I'll have to put you in another group, Bailey bridging instead of mine detection.' I said, 'All right.'

I come back to do Bailey bridging. I've left my haversack, with my music in, and my mattress in the hut they've transferred me to. Getting near to lights out I'm looking for them, looking, looking. A voice says, 'It's up there!' Just as I look up, a corporal calls, 'Lights out!' All my stuff had been put in a bundle and tied up to hang by a kind of pulley-rope over a beam in the middle of the hut. I said, 'Lights out be blowed! I'm taking my stuff down!' Another corporal came in. 'Oh, *you're* back!' I'd never seen the man in my life. The Cohen story must have spread during a beer session in the Corporals'

Mess. 'Yes,' I said, 'and I'm just getting my equipment which some happy people have put up there.' He said, 'You'll have to try and do it in the dark. I'll be seeing you in the morning.'

I was pulled up before the Company Major. I explained the circumstances. I said, 'I've heard of army discipline, but the corporal's pushing it, isn't he?!' He said, 'Maybe the boys were just playing a joke.' I said, 'What?! On a person they haven't seen before?!' He couldn't answer.

I took a violent dislike to the people in that hut right away. I don't like jokes from people that don't know me. I asked could I be transferred to another hut. They said, 'But you're now on the Bailey bridging.' I said, 'Is there no other company or section doing Bailey bridging? If not, transfer me back to mine detection!' While the Company Major was hum-ing and ha-ing, I maintained an icy indifference in the hut. The boys were all raw novices. I was ignoring them, I wouldn't speak, and there's a tradition that senior soldiers give the others a bit of a tip about blancoing, how to clean a rifle and how to place your stuff down in the morning for inspection. Well, the corporals were having to show them and I was doing my own business and didn't want to know. It caused a bit of antagonism. One word led to another and some nice chap from Dorset finished up fighting me in the toilets. There were no spectators. I said, 'I don't want your mob jumping on me when I'm facing you. If we're going in there, we're going in alone!' He said, 'Who's to stop you putting in the boot?' I said, 'Well, let's put on the slippers! And no belts!' We had a go. Then I had a go with his mate, a Scotsman who took umbrage. It just grew. I'd a fight every night and twice on Saturdays for two weeks. I had to win because, if one of them would have beaten me, I'd have lost respect. Reports were coming through to the major from the corporals and the sergeants involved in the training that too many boys were coming to parade with black eyes, busted noses and split lips. The order was, 'Get him out of the hut!' I was sent from B Company right over to E Company, still Bailey bridging which I never had any use for.

After my three months' training as a sapper, they sent me for six weeks up into the Highlands. The company was blasting granite for making quays for the invasion barges. My detail was to take the blunted bits of the drills to the blacksmith for re-sharpening. But I had a skirmish while I was there with a major organizing a concert party, the first of a series of shows which was to come to a climax in a big theatre in Sauchiehall Street or Queen Street, I forget which, in the middle of Glasgow.

The evening of the concert I didn't feel too fresh after a day's blasting up in the mountains. Nevertheless, after a late tea, at about half past five, about thirty of us got in a coach and went off to a hall to entertain some Poles. I must say this for the Scottish—they were always prepared to entertain the continentals. Well, I was singing one of my stock ballads—'For You Alone'—when the accompanist, who was an ATS captain and a lover of a Scottish sergeant, a tenor singing 'The Holy City' in the same programme, dropped the middle sheet of my music during my performance. I stopped and said to the audience, 'Don't worry! We'll commence operations again in a moment!' I wasn't trying to belittle her. When she'd found the music, I carried on. She put the poison in afterwards by telling the major I'd taken the mickey. He said to me, 'You insulted the pianist!' I said, 'Sir, she *did* drop the music! I tried to help her by covering up!' He said, 'You should have remembered her rank! You should have dived for the music!' I said, 'Sir, when I'm on the stage, *I*'m in charge!'

Then because I spoke for the men to the major about the badly cooked food, I was sent from the Highlands down to Bradford on a course on bulldozer, lorry and tank repair work with MERE, the mechanical equipment section of the Royal Engineers. I arrived at this building, part barracks, part canteen. I was homesick again. I was lonely, I was among strangers, I had been shifted around from one place to another, I had no friends. I ordered sausages and chips and a cup of tea and two slices. Behind the counter was a big, good-looking North-country-woman, fortyish, from the WVS. She was sympathetic. She began chatting to me. I told her I was a Londoner and did a bit of singing. Do you know, I finished up singing half a dozen songs for her?! There must have been twenty soldiers eating in the canteen, and three other women serving behind the counter. Everybody clapped. 'Shine through my dreams' they particularly liked. It was a nice memento of my stay in Bradford. I've often wished I could live in the North. A different type of people to Londoners entirely. They're friendly people.

After three months in Bradford, I was sent to RE HQ in Balham for a day where I was upgraded from PSE (Pioneer Sapper Engineer) 5 to PSE 3, and then sent to a kind of Manor House near Bishop's Stortford where I stayed for three or four weeks. There, ironically, I was made a sweeper, the lowest job a man could be given in the RE's, because, despite being a PSE 3, I hadn't finished any training and therefore wasn't a specialist.

The rations of about two hundred men were coming in, yet there were only fifty or sixty men on the post. Mind you, I got plenty to eat. Our cook used to work in the Savoy before the war and, apart from our rations of stew or roast beef and rice and custard, he prepared rabbits, pheasants and partridges, shot by the second in command for officers and friends, of which I got my share because I did some spud-bashing for him occasionally and I also used to drop him a couple of bob. The sleeping and eating conditions were the best I'd had since I left the Infantry and there was no antagonism. But who wants to sweep corridors and bedrooms and hide in the lavatories so the officers who know you haven't got any work can't see you? And the men were only concerned with their own little number, they had their own little groups set up and I was too late to be enrolled. I soon got depressed. This place was a dead end. I became a recluse. I hardly ever spoke and, when I did, I stammered. I began to suffer from nightmares in the rare moments I could even doze off. I was reliving the fighting, antagonism and hatred I had endured in those God knows how many units I'd passed through. I asked to see the major. He was an Irish major. I said that I'd like to be sent somewhere for treatment. 'But you're a brave boy!' he said. 'Your race is a fighting race! You've got to snap out of this!' I said, 'When you've had as many fights as I have over nothing but your religion and your face, it does become a bit of a bore!' He put the necessary procedure in motion, I saw a psychiatrist in Colchester and finished up in the Psychiatric Unit of Mill Hill Emergency Hospital.

I stayed there for six weeks. The psychiatrist was a German Jew. The first time I met him, he asked me did I feel any better than when I came. I said, 'Yes. There are less restrictions. I feel better physically. But mentally—no. My fits of depression haven't eased off.' He said, 'Why not go into the *tailoring* section of the army?' I said, 'There's no tailoring section *in* the army!' As I talked to him I was crying. Just the idea of being associated with the army made me sick. We were supposed to be friends fighting the enemy, and I was fed up with the physical and mental effort of being with people who were either hostile or indifferent. I just wanted out. He told me I was suffering from a persecution complex. He tried to make me see that, out of hundreds of thousands of decent people, I had come across a few bastards who thought it a duty to remind me forcibly that, though I was born and bred in England, I was a dirty Jew. The second and last time we met—September, 1943—he discharged me and suggested I apply to the War Office for a disability pension. I didn't.

On my discharge papers was written: 'Lack of moral fibre'. What a laugh! For twenty-one months I'd not only to confine myself to the ballad class of music of the United Kingdom and deny myself the pleasures of singing the unpatriotic Italian and German songs I enjoyed, I'd to fight my so-called friends, allies and fellow-countrymen instead of fighting the so-called enemy! I went straight back on the demolition with Griffiths, clearing bomb damage, boarding-up, making it safe for people to walk along Commercial Road, Whitechapel Road, Grays Inn Road . . .

One day we were in a square in St Mary Axe, breaking the stone slabs of two damaged buildings into manageable pieces with picks and seven pound hammers and putting them onto the lorry, when, during a tea break, a few of us—me, Fat Barney and Joe Bananas—took it in turn to sing a song. I sang 'For You Alone' and was amazed at the end of it to hear twenty or thirty people applauding like mad on a roof more than a hundred yards away across the square. I bowed like a true Thespian and sang two or three songs more. I was so encouraged that, still being a patriot of a dubious kind, I decided to do my bit by joining ENSA. I filled in a form and received an answer that I was to go for an audition in a flea-pit theatre, whose name I forget, in the West End. A friend of mine, Danny Samson, drove me there in his taxi. I sang 'Shine through my dreams' or another stand-by, but I wasn't a comedian or a young girl of twenty who could kick her legs up, so I didn't hear any more.

I carried on doing the demolition till the hard winter of '45–'46 when there was such a freeze-up that most work stopped for four or five months and, instead of earning a tenner a week, I'd to go back into tailoring as an improver hand with Mr Hirsh who had opened another workshop during the war in Turner Street. Here we go round again!

I stayed with Mr Hirsh as an improver tailor from 1946 to 1948, without any change in my weekly wage of five pound ten. Then began the period of the busy and slack times in the tailoring trade. You were employed during the busy seasons—March to June or July, and October to January—and walking around during the slack. Between 1948 and 1952 I worked for as many as a dozen unappreciative guvnors who made their own busy and slack and filled their pockets at my expense and thought they were doing me a favour. 1949 was the worst year tailoring had ever seen. In that year I only worked in January and February. I'd to take a barrow at week-ends and try to sell my own paperbacks—science fiction, detective stories, boxing books—on the Whitechapel Waste.

In 1950/51 I became an under presser for the first time—with a gents' tailors called Green and Black. An under presser presses all the pieces of a garment—the foreparts, the back, the collar, the pocket flaps and the sleeves—on the wrong side. Then, when they're joined up, he presses the seams that connect them—all on the wrong side. In those days I used a sixteen pound gas (or 'goose') hand iron and a damp rag. Since 1951 I've used an electric steam iron, also sixteen pounds, no damp rag. A gas iron has got to be changed every two or three minutes, and a rag has got to be damped forty to fifty times a day. With an electric steam iron I get the steam direct from the boiler and can produce more with less effort. I was worried the first time I started to work with one, but now I wouldn't use anything else. They're a lot quicker and easier.

In former years there was a snobbery involving the difference between a top presser and an under presser, and a big difference in their wages. Today their value is recognized as the same and their wages are the same. The man who now cops the cream is the Hoffman presser. The Hoffman is a big machine, with two large pads, that steams the material after it's cut to take out any gloss and pre-shrink it, and presses the foreparts and backs in sections, the bulk work or 'body', as it's called, when the garment is made up. It's a dirty business. I'd never be a Hoffman presser for five times the money. With the intense heat and steam, man-made fibres give off large clouds of chemical vapour which get in your eyes, your nose, your guts. They don't pay you big wages for nothing. I at least can control the amount of steam I use.

In 1951 I moved to J. Cinna, tailoring ladies' mantles, and I've never been back to gents' since—the money's better. In 1952 I went in to Mr Lefcovitch in Ashfield Street and asked for a job as an under presser at £12 a week. He gave it to me and, believe me, in 1952 £12 was a bloody good wage. I doubt if a top presser would have got more than £16. Though I was sometimes on a three and a half day week, I worked for that man for five years, and I didn't have to ask for a single rise as there was no change in the cost of living. Then he died and his son couldn't continue at a profit. Between 1958 and 1964 I worked for about twenty more different guvnors, still as an under presser and only accepting a minimum of £15 a week.

One mild day in 1964, after a long lay-off, I walked down Commercial Road and looked along either side to see if there were any vacancies. There were none. I was going home to dinner through New Road, and I was walking on the left hand side where the factories are, when I noticed a sign in the window of Beverly Sportswear saying UNDER PRESSER WANTED. I went inside and was greeted by a middle-aged man, the elder brother and partner of Isaac Lustigman, the top guvnor. He took me by the arm and guided me up a flight of stairs and pointed to a door on the left hand side of a small landing. 'Knock there!' Behind that door I found three people I'd worked with before, using steam irons at a pressing table. Supervising them was the quiet and unassuming Mr Issy Lustigman. He said, 'Take your coat off!' and at the end of the day he asked, 'What do you want, chaver (that means 'comrade' in Hebrew)?' and

I said, '£16' and I've been with him ever since, that's ten years, and, please God, I'll have the strength to work for him for another ten or twenty.

Mr Lustigman's not one of the tight merchants, he's fair. He's part manufacturer, part outdoor worker. At the end of my first two years he gave me a £1 rise. That disappeared in tax, so he gave me another pound in about six months. Since then, I've been going to him every year and getting £2 more. If things don't level up and stop spiralling, he'll probably give me £3, which, after tax, will work out at two. I hope I'll continue to be worth it to him. He once called me the pillar of his business. He's the first person I've ever worked for who's a real gentleman. Once in a while, if I oversleep myself, there's no shouting, he just comes along to where I live and bangs on my door. We're like friends. At night I help him to lock up and make sure all the lights and irons are off and keep him company as it's a very dark and gloomy building.

The firm is called Beverly Sportswear after Mr Lustigman's daughter, Beverly. The 'Sportswear' was a pipe-dream of one of the partners, and all we actually make is women's coats and costumes. It's a family atmosphere. We always seem to be celebrating births and marriages and other happy occasions. Whatever the event, it's recorded by the people of the workshop having a drink and saying, 'L'chayim!' ('To life!')—normally with scotch for the men and cherry brandy for the women. I must have had at least a thousand drinks over the years. But the guvnors are very practical! They don't like to break up the sequence of work, so a celebration comes about ten minutes to a quarter of an hour before dinner-time. Whoever is arranging it goes to the big tailors' table, which has a run of about thirty feet, and puts down all the drink and plava cake. Then, come dinner-time, everybody joins him, not in a mad rush, very leisurely in fact, but with a determined effort to get to that table for their share.

There are only two drawbacks about working for Issy Lustigman apart from the pace. One is that the heat in the workshop is too intense. The other is that the chemicals in the fibres give off a vapour which cuts down the oxygen. So, to keep fit, I have to eat well, sleep well and observe some simple hygienic rules:

When I get up I have a couple of sips of water to clear the mouth. I then have a cup of tea down the road, or else go straight to the workshop where I always make myself a cup before starting at eight. Ten to ten, I have two cups of tea. When a couple of the girls objected because everyone else has only one, the boss said, 'He deserves it,' and now buys an extra bottle of milk so they can't hide the milk and make the excuse I have too much. He knows that the better he looks after me, the better I work. I have a couple of cakes with my tea out of what I buy from Rinkoff's on Fridays, for myself and my sister, Betty, a selection of brown bread, pletsls, fairy cakes, honey cake, flat cheesecakes with raisins on top, square cheesecakes with sugar on top, doughnuts and cream éclairs. They only charge me 70p. I'm a Yiddisher boy, a bachelor and a friend of the family. They say to themselves, 'Why sling them into the waste-bin for the pigs or make bread pudding when we can charge Alex 70p?' They're nice people but they're realists. For dinner—and for me it's a snack—I have, say, soup, spaghetti bolognese, rice and custard and a cup of tea, or soup, two eggs and bacon, two slices of bread and butter, rice and custard and a cup of tea. Come tea-time, ten to four, I have a couple more cups of tea and two cakes. Half past five, I walk out the door and make my way very quickly to some café for supper, my main meal—soup, if possible, a main course, sweet and two teas. When I get home, I have a bowel evacuation, then eat two big cheese sandwiches, a bar of chocolate, a few sherbet lemons and a bit of cake with a pint and a half of tea. My body wants the nourishment. Food with me doesn't turn to fat, it just restores lost energy. About ten o'clock, I have a second evacuation and, about five minutes before getting into bed, I roll a corner of my handkerchief into a point and tickle the inside of my nostrils to make me sneeze and clear the rubbish that's accumulated during the day in my nose and head.

FIVE

The Maccabi Association is international. It's made up of Jewish clubs whose intention it is to combine friendship, the arts, sport and the normal pursuits so as to give its members a rounded outlook on life, make them into decent citizens worthy of the Jewish people, and prepare them in case of trouble to protect themselves not by way of arms but by physical fitness. The name 'Maccabi' was taken from Judas the Maccabee, the leader of the Jewish resistance in Israel at the time of the Syrian occupation. In 1932, the Association helped a lot of German and Austrian Jews get out of Germany on the pretext that they were competing in the Olympic Games in Los Angeles.

During the war, some Jewish East Enders grew so friendly in the Underground shelters that they decided to try to continue the relationship afterwards. They approached the headquarters of the Maccabi in Compayne Gardens and were given a building in Deal Street. So began the East London Maccabi, and I became a member of it at the time I started working again for Mr Hirsh.

The building in Deal Street was very large with twenty-six or twenty-eight rooms, including a hall with a stage and a big gymnasium, but unfortunately we had no furniture or equipment. Cleaning up, curtaining, painting, decorating, began at once. Fifty or sixty chairs and a few tables were found to set up a canteen and we made do there while we prepared for a fund-raising concert to be given at the Jewish Palais in the Commercial Road. Jack Rogers and his wife, Muriel, were in charge. Muriel's sister was the pianist. We got together singers, script-writers, ideas men and two or three comedians which included

Ronnie Fingers and Sid and Manny Cohen, and gradually built up a programme. I was to sing 'Shine Through My Dreams' and the 'Serenade' from *The Student Prince*, and I remember that the opening sketch was a preview of the show, with me holding my nose and pulling a chain, someone else holding an umbrella, pretending there was a leak in the roof—snide and quick-moving remarks and gestures like that.

My family had never been to any of the concerts I did at the Toynbee, so I asked my mother along, and she dragged in the rest—Morry and his wife Milly, Steve and his wife Kitty, and Reggie and Alan and Jack. They all, as you might say, presented a solid front for me in the middle of the hall. Three or four hundred people were there. The man who put on Yiddisher plays at the Jewish Palais had sneaked a few of the tickets for his own artists. It was a very nice atmosphere and a very successful evening. We took over £120 on the tickets and there were quite a number of donations, £180 odd we made altogether. Now we could buy a piano and so on, and the Maccabi Association were shamed into pitching in with gym equipment and a record player. The place began to move.

We were a very useful, progressive group of people. We had discussions, weight-lifting, socials. Mr Beresford, who had a shop in Aldgate called Levy's, used to come up on a Tuesday night and play gramophone records of opera and popular music. We gave a series of concert parties, and not only to people inside the Association. One was in the middle of 1946, the severest winter since 1942, in a synagogue way out in Gantshill. I walked out onto the stage wearing my hat, my overcoat and my scarf, and nobody laughed because everyone in the audience was wrapped up too. And who was in that audience but Mr and Mrs Rosenthal, the parents of my friend, Sidney, who was killed tragically in an air crash during the war. Which reminds me there was *another* death of a boy I knew. Also in an air crash. But one tragedy on a page is enough. I hate to see our people go!

The discussions—always on a Monday—were chaired by a little man, a professional debater, who'd ask a few questions, then say, 'Let's talk tonight about the economy', or 'Let's talk tonight about politics as they affect the working man.' He set us all alight. He awakened our minds and kept them sharp. We were like a House of Commons. We had members who were true blue conservatives and we had the working class. I always found myself talking for the Unions and the working class—that's what *I* was, working class. Sometimes we got a bit heated, but this was taken in good part and in friendliness. Subjects were never taken to a vote, but if one side had made a good point this was recognized. An important issue of the time was 'Should Great Britain adopt the same tactics of surveillance over Communists as the Americans?'

I took up weight-lifting because I didn't want to get too slack physically after the fitness I'd acquired through necessity in the army. I did it for its own sake, that is, I used to train for strength, and the shape followed. The rest trained for shape, and if the strength followed it was a surprise. One of our chaps won the Mr Universe, Class Two (Medium Height)—Mark Lewis, who was five foot seven. An Egyptian won the Main Title. He was six foot. I'd get a bar of about two hundred and fifty pounds on my shoulders and do the deep knee bend till I was squatting, then stand up. I did it five or six times, then rested. The exercise itself is good, but the rest in between is more beneficial. That was why we worked in groups. It gave you time to breathe. On that routine I worked up to just under four hundred pounds. I also did the dead lift—French style and hack style. The French style involved reverse hand grips. Hack style I never liked—I didn't want to change my sex at that late date. You had to put the bar between your legs and pull it up till it reached the crutch.

Weight-lifting led to putting the shot, throwing the discus, a bit of wrestling, a bit of swimming, a bit of running. My friends were all-round sportsmen. I went off with them. I was young. I was experimenting. I was never backward in coming forward to try new ways of mixing with people. Half a dozen of us had just finished doing the athletics somewhere down in Hackney one afternoon, and someone who knew a Scotch girl on the bash in the back doubles fancied a short time. She charged us half a quid each for a knee trembler. I found something out: I'm not at my best after running three miles around a track. I didn't enjoy it. I made a promise that I'd never go with a prostitute again.

Women are a question of time and luck. If there would have been a working-class girl with some smattering of music or art I might have married her. Two people have to get along. Sex is only part of it. I was looking for a Jewish girl, not necessarily as wonderful as Nettie, but with an amiable disposition and passable looks. Two out of three would do. Never found her. I've known many, many girls—good-looking, plain-looking, intelligent, stupid. I was friendly with all of them, and there were one or two that I fancied so I chanced my arm, but I wasn't for them. I have to admit this handicap—girls who are really good-looking with good figures and lovely faces have never wanted me. Once my main purpose in life was to make a career as a singer, and they say that an artist has only one mistress and that's his art. But the greatest artists in the world get lonely in bed. You don't go through life singing all the time. I'd like to have married. I'd like to have a wife and children. Sometimes I wake up in the middle of the night and I'm alone and I don't like it. But there's nothing for it but to just hang on and to keep on living.

The East London Maccabi was mixed. The girls were intellectual types. I didn't get along with most of them because they *were* intellectual, and those I liked were too good-looking and they didn't fancy me, and those that fancied me were plain and I can't stand a plain woman. In one respect we were unlike a lot of other clubs. In them you were allowed to dance the waltz or foxtrot or tango but if anybody tried to do a bit of jitterbugging they were hauled off the floor. Not with us. During the six years I was there, a certain amount of jitterbugging and rock and roll was allowed. There was no lack of morals or decorum yet everybody had a good time. All girls go to a club to be picked up, and all boys go there for the sake of picking them up. We didn't pretend that whoever was taking somebody home was just going to see her to the door and say goodnight. But that was none of our business. Anyhow, very few Jewish boys and girls, whether they're going to get married or not, and even if they're unorthodox and almost without religion, will go to bed with one another before marriage, though they'll do it with a Gentile. And we don't have many mixed marriages. It's bad enough that she's a girl and he's a boy. A boy's got troubles enough already. A girl doesn't think the same. She doesn't feel the same. She feels more than she thinks and a boy thinks more than he feels, or at least he feels at only one point.

Very occasionally we'd have a Jewish girl with hot pants. There was one girl, and we knew she was a flirt. A few boys had taken her out, and boys talk. Well, this nice, quiet, studious type of boy began to take her out. I said, 'I hope you're not getting too serious with that girl. I don't know if it's true, but she's got a reputation.' He said, 'We're getting married next month.' I heard the clang. I met him after they were married and I apologized in a fashion. I said, 'I'm very sorry if I said anything that was uncalled for, but I was only speaking to your benefit. Are you happy?' He said, 'Yes.' She was that rare Jewish girl who is a hot pants. Most Jewish girls if they meet a nice fellow —nice way of talking, decently dressed, not a pig—are content to wait, but this one liked to sample the goods as well. Her future husband didn't hear about it from any of the others and I slipped. But there was no umbrage, no deep-seated feeling about 'What's he interfering for!'—that was what was so nice about the club. And apparently they were very, very happy. The girl had found something more than a randy boy to satisfy her.

During the summer we used to go on coach trips to Margate and Bognor Regis. You need never be alone if you belong to a club. We had some marvellous times. We used to be singing there and back. Me personally when I got there, I took off the shirt and sat in the sun and chatted up the birds. There was one incident at Bognor. I was playing quoits with some of the girls. Suddenly a big, hulking brute comes along looking for an argument and says, 'You're disturbing the kids!' I said, 'What are you getting excited about? We're at the seaside. We're playing.' Well, I weighed him up and he weighed me up. All I was wearing was a pair of shorts and I looked like a muscular man. He swallowed.

One Sunday evening in the March or April of 1946 when I was first beginning to settle into the club, four or five men appeared, led by an ex-paratrooper who had served in Arnhem and had won the MM. He'd already been round the other East End clubs and was raising a company of Jewish ex-servicemen to fight the emerging Fascists. His second in command came too—

he is now a top name in a big national newspaper and was then an organizer of the *On Guard*, the weekly paper issued by the group which was called the 43 Group because, the story goes, he and the leader and a few friends booked a room next to where the Fascists were meeting and the number of that room was 43. The 43 Group's plan was not only to expose the Fascist detainees who had been sent to the Isle of Wight during the war and were now released, but also the Fascists who were communicating with one another through their Book Clubs. Mosley was in the background, it was rumoured, waiting for Burgess and Hamm and others to build the movement up again to the strength of the British Union of Fascists before the war. They even intended to put forty or fifty candidates in the field for the 1950 election. In essence we were asked to prevent pre-war Fascism from raising its head again. Before the war, apart from a few nutty intellectuals, the Fascists contained quite a lot of the poor working class who for half a quid to a pound a time would bash anybody. They didn't change much after the war. I don't even think they hated the Jews. It was a chance for idiots to pick up money, mix with people and work out their frustrations. We were worried about the clever ones, the ones who wanted power.

Half a dozen of us, including three ex-army privates and one ex-naval rating, joined the Group. We were asked if we owned cars. Two did. We turned up at another club which shall be nameless—though I don't want everyone to think Clubland is a centre of espionage and intrigue—and found forty to fifty strong boys like ourselves.

There were about seven London contingents altogether. We were the East End contingent. The combined fighting contingent for the whole of London—the shock troops, the assault troops, the strong arm stuff—came to just on three hundred. There was also a Representative Planning Group of about ten, and another three hundred or so, male and female, for Security and Intelligence. The fighting contingent had a fleet of cars and small vans which could transport its members to any part of London you care to mention in five minutes. One Sunday we set up a record. We turned over thirteen meetings all in the space of about three hours. We didn't argue. We didn't ask questions. We just moved into a thing, turned over the platform, gave a few Blackshirts a beating and kicked them up the arse. We always wore a white shirt—it didn't matter if it was under a jacket—so that we could recognize one another, and we didn't carry any personal papers but put them in an envelope for collecting when we got back to Central HQ in the West End.

I was only once in danger. The Communists were good talkers but hadn't the belly for a fight. We broke up a meeting which the Fascists were holding in a side street by the Classic Cinema, Dalston, and came back to Ridley Road to guard a Communist meeting from attack. More than a thousand Fascists were across the road looking all sorts of daggers at us. The Communist meeting began to break up. I made the mistake of allowing myself to get separated from the Group. The next thing I knew was that a little old man hiding in the doorway of a pub hit me on the back of the head with a brick. I gave him a push and he went bowling over. Right away I heard, 'Look! He's started on old Charlie!' and about a dozen young men began to come round me. The Group were by now forty or sixty yards down the road. I put my back up against a lamp-post and slung my arms about doing the long arm punches like a fighting dervish. Thank God for my powerful voice. I shouted, 'Help!' and a dozen of our big boys ran back towards me and, as soon as they started to hit a couple of these little bully boys, they turned and ran away.

We knew that there were about a thousand Fascists in London and that they outnumbered us by about four to one. But they didn't know *our* figures. Our Intelligence had a Jewish girl who didn't look Jewish and who penetrated right into the heart of the Fascist organization and could give us all their movements and figures, even the movements and figures of their splinter groups. Her cover was a Christian anti-Fascist. We were not above pretending to be policemen, either. Some of our big chaps, chosen because they didn't look Jewish, paid a visit to Hamm's home, knocked on his door and, when he opened it, said that they were Special Police and that they'd like to look at his books and pamphlets. They ransacked the place, put a lot of his stuff in a hold-all and said, 'We'll look through all this at the Yard and then return it to you.' Of course they never did.

We who began the movement were genuine with good intentions, but it finished up as a business, a lousy business. Though rich and influential Jews were supporting us with funds, we never got our expenses. The money that was coming into the coffers was not accounted for. Also my character was being affected. I couldn't get on a bus or a train or walk in the street as I do today. I was very much on edge. I was always watching who was a Jew and who was a Christian, and who was for me, who against me. I was on guard like the name of our paper. I was living on my nerves. I was like a saboteur. We had broken up so many Fascist meetings that we were having to hide, we could no longer come out onto the streets. When trouble began to brew in the Middle East in 1948, a meeting was held at which it was suggested that a number of us might like to volunteer to serve in the Israeli army. I right away said No, I'd done my share in the army and I'd be away from my mother who wasn't a youngster. Two or three years earlier, Bernie Simmons, a friend of mine at the Settlement—a social club in Buxton Street with Zionist tendencies which included several of our old Habonim members—had said to me, 'Why don't you come with us to Israel, Alex?' I answered in a way which, looking back, shows I wasn't an idiot. I said, 'Idealism is all right, but I'm a working man. I don't mind being a working man here, but I won't take the same gaff in Israel, I won't work for any capitalist out there. The fact that he's a Jewish capitalist won't make me any happier. Here I know where I am. In Israel I won't know.' Yet about a hundred Jewish boys and girls went out to Israel to make their own kibbutz, and in 1948 a large number of the British-Jewish Legion and the Board of Deputies as well as members of the 43 Group went out to fight in the Jewish-Arab War.

I eased out of the Group. After the Arab-Israel War of '48 had been through the motions I met some friends. They had been through the formality of getting to France and throwing away their passports so as to go through Europe to Sicily as Displaced Persons and then charter a boat to Israel, but they were hardly clear of the ship in Calais when they were arrested and put into a special French prison till the war was over. Quite a number of people are looking for the man who blew the plan, the same man as made off with our expenses. There isn't an equivalent of the 43 Group today. Instead, local groups of observers inform the Jewish Board of Deputies and the Jewish Board of Guardians and the Jewish Ex-Servicemen's associations of any resurgence of Fascist activities, for example, the activities of the National Front.

In the past the English people were either for or against the Fascists, or for or against the Jews. But in the 1973 Arab-Israel conflict they showed themselves to be strangely indifferent. In my view there's too much pacifism about. Pacifism's dangerous. Be committed one way or the other. By being a pacifist, by doing nothing, you are being as anti-Semitic as the violent ones. I say to those who ask me why *I* don't go to fight for the Jews abroad that someone has to stay behind to tell the English that they're making this mistake!

Fortunately here in the East End the Jews are no longer the target of Fascist jibes. Anti-Semitism, not only as reflected in the Fascists but in the ignorant cockney, has now been directed towards the 'dirty black bastards' and 'the Pakistani gits'. Instead of the middle-class and more refined Jews, who moved out of the East End to Dalston, Stamford Hill, Forest Gate, Golders Green, Cricklewood and Gantshill, are the Jamaicans and the Pakistanis. As soon as they came, the Fascists said, 'We don't need the Jews any more. They're overplayed, they're overworked.' So for the past fifteen or sixteen years no Fascist meeting talks about us. Mind you we're still the ace in their hole, but we're no more their big enemy. Now it's the coloured immigrants. Poor sods! I pity them!

Because I'm a Jew, because I've been through a bit of this kind of trouble myself, I want to say something about the coloured immigrants from a humanitarian point of view. When they came here, they came with hatred in their hearts, they said that they'd been exploited. Somebody ought to explain to them that the white people of this country were exploited just as much as they were. The Establishment here, who had their representatives abroad, *they* took the cream, *they* raped these countries, the working class didn't. And, now the chickens have come home to roost, who is supporting them? The average ratepayer, the average working man who gets taxed whether he likes it or not. And who are we workers keeping? People who think we are the people who exploited them because we are the only people they see. Yet we are victims the same as them. They've come in like an invading army and they will not integrate. The Jews were proud to come to this country. They set up little businesses and there is no racial prejudice in a Jewish firm—whether you're Jew, Gentile, black, white, green, Martian, Venus, the Moon, most Jewish guvnors, not all, will pay you a living wage, unlike the typical English guvnor who thinks he's doing you a big favour if he employs you and if you work for him for sixty hours a week he might give you survival pay. The Jews are now integrated with the British people. We are patriotic. We are loyal. We are law-abiding citizens. Ask for the prison records of the Jewish population of the United Kingdom. The figures would amaze you. Thieving is for people who have got no brains or are lazy. Jews have always worked. England has had the benefit of their trades and they have set new standards in the City. Yet many of the coloured people are behaving like parasites with resentment in their hearts and at the same time breeding like rabbits, while the English, determined to destroy their national identity are advocating vasectomy, the pill and Women's Lib. Maybe what we want is less Assistance and more Jewish guvnors running Industry. If they wanted workers they'd pay for them, and to increase production they'd get the latest machinery, use time and motion experts, put the workers on production bonuses and get the Government not to be so greedy as to tax the nuts off them whenever they earn extra money. If you're earning money you don't care if the work's dull and repetitious, not if you can live outside working hours as a middle-class citizen. There should be no need for overtime when you're working full pace and earning £100 a week like in America—overtime should be cream. You could have two shifts—the first from eight in the morning till four in the afternoon—work right through, no break. The second shift would last from six o'clock till two in the morning. If you want to be greedier, have three shifts, but that would abuse the machines. The trouble with the English guvnor is that he has a misguided sense of superiority. He thinks that, because he makes big money and lives the high and good life, the people who work for him are idiots and should be conned and taken for a ride. He forgets that *he* is the parasite and that they are the breadwinners for him and themselves. When you degrade workers, you take away from them the idea of a professional standard, the idea of wanting to be of the highest ability in your trade or craft and worthy of the best income you can get as your due because you are making the country rich. How can you expect a worker to be patriotic if you don't give him any incentive to be patriotic?

It isn't that Jewish employers are more humane. I don't think they are. It's just that most of them are more practical and more approachable as well. One Jew I knew treated his workers as numbers in a grand system, namely, a syndicate of ten or a dozen firms. Myself and another under presser did what was necessary for the tailor and the special machinists and, without knowing it, pushed up production more than twenty-five per cent in about three months. We did four hundred coats a day. For the one thousand five hundred coats he had before, he was getting two thousand a week. He congratulated us. It was in 1960 and we were getting £16 a week. I said, 'Well, there's only one way you can show your appreciation—with money in the packet.' 'Oh,' he said, 'I don't pay any under presser more than £16 a week!' Within two weeks I'd left the job.

In the early fifties I was sitting down in the canteen of the East London Maccabi with a couple of friends, and there seemed to be nothing but kids of sixteen and seventeen dancing and talking around us, so we began to count heads. We were boys looking for girls, and the girls were too young! We decided to join the Mile End Old Boys' at 241, Mile End Road which catered for the ages of eighteen up to fifty and let in girls for dancing at a great profit on Wednesdays and Sundays only. The only drawback about those dances was that some of the senior members had a habit of going to the pub two doors away. They'd have a good old drink up and come back a bit on the noisy side about their admiration for the younger girls.

At the Mile End Old Boys' I became cricket scorer and, as first aid man for the football, I had a principle which everyone now recognizes—if a person's dazed, you slap a wet sponge at the back of his neck and that revives him. I was also able to continue with my weight-lifting. Sometimes at the end of a work-out I felt a little bit tight and tired, but there was always a bottle of oil handy, so I gave myself a good rub and quivered my shoulders and shook my arms and rolled them over and over. As I've said before, I exercised for strength and not for shape. The principle was to tear down the muscular tissue which then came back to normal overnight with a little bit more tensile strength. It gave me an enormous appetite. I once did an experiment during dinner. I had some chopped liver and a couple of slices of bread, then I took my bar which had about a hundred and fifty pounds on it and I pressed it above my head four or five times. Then I sat down again and had a plate of soup. I do a few reps with dumb-bells, sixty, seventy pounds each. I go through the whole list. The piece of fish—a few deep knee bends with the bar, two hundred pounds. Braised steak followed by side to side pressing. Apple strudel—dumb-bells and hip movements. At the end of forty-five minutes to an hour when I'd gone through the whole meal apart from the cup of tea, my mother comes in with a pot and I say very seriously, 'Mum, is there any chance I could have some more dinner?' I was starving!

But it's for singing that I remember the club most of all. The building loved my voice. Right away, Mr Harry Stanger, who was not only Chairman of the club but also choreographer of the Old Stepnians' Operatic Society which I later joined, said, 'Don't use the mike. It's no good for you. Your voice could fill the Albert Hall.' So I never used the microphone at all, but because that building so loved my voice the people below playing snooker and weight-lifting could hear me and the people three floors up playing table-tennis could hear me too. No one else's voice behaved in that way, but mine just spread all over the building.

I was in my singing prime. One Saturday evening at about seven I was practising Ponchielli's 'Cielo e mar' very softly in the No. 18, Carter House. There was a top note, a B flat. Because of the people upstairs I couldn't do what I normally did so I placed the note in the head. The bel canto method! Forget all the other bad ways of singing! If you want the voice to be full and in the front mask, the front of the head and not the back of the head which is the sounding-board, what you do is this—you pitch the note to the back and it rebounds to the front, but the higher you go you must pitch it towards the crown of the head till the voice doesn't seem to come from the face at all, it's somehow about six inches above you. That is how you sing the golden notes. It was a step forward I should have taken years previously.

At the Mile End Old Boys' we were always putting on concerts, sometimes at the club and sometimes on tour, sometimes to raise money for ourselves, sometimes to raise money for hospitals, old age pensioners and other charities. I carried at least a dozen songs around with me—three for the show, two or three for encores and emergencies, and the rest for padding out the suitcase. *The Two Four One*, the club magazine, says this about the concert parties in 1956: 'Alex Hartog needs no introduction. He's singing more encores than his listed programme.' Because of those repeated encores I just had to announce my own songs and I found to my delight that my stammer gradually went away in that friendly atmosphere where my singing was appreciated.

I was versatile. One lot of the boys I mixed with were conscious of their figures, of their movements, of their sweating, of what to eat, what to drink. We were working for a better physique or more strength or both. With others it was how to make a rounded bill, how to present a show. I had different interests and therefore different sorts of friends. They were all my friends, but if I was to introduce the weight-lifters to the singers they would have looked at one another aghast and wouldn't have known what to say. As regards sex, the club contained a few married men and a lot of bachelors. We knew who the homosexuals were but none of them stepped out of line. There was this understanding—club boys as companions, but keep politics and sex for afterwards; in the club only sport and music; if you're a homosexual, or if you're a Communist and you want to blow up England, all right so long as you don't want to bring it in and speak about it; so it's a mad world outside, but why not keep the unity of the club?

Mr Lefcovitch died the night before I was to appear in a show for the London Jewish Hospital. I said to his son, 'I hope you don't take umbrage, but your father had a very funny way of avoiding hearing me sing!' Another time there was to be rather a special concert on a Sunday. Instead of performing on our stage, we were going to turn the hall into a night club with a piano on the floor. A very nice girl I met while singing at the Porchester Hotel for a Jewish club called 'The Three S's' invited me to go on a coach trip that day. I said, 'I've a concert to do.' Over the years I've thought, 'You bloody idiot! For a lousy stinking concert you gave up a nice friendly girl who was looking for a husband!'

After an Emergency General Meeting in 1964 or '65, the building was sold to Queen Mary's College as a rest centre for students, and the Jewish Lads' Brigade, who were occupying three rooms at the top and had proposed to buy the property or pay for half of it to the Mile End Old Boys' Association, were kicked out too. I was furious.

I still am. Never mind our members, thirty years old and upwards, what about the JLB who wanted to buy in? An important part of life to youngsters was cut out of their system. At a club you learn how to live with people and get along with people. Certain rules of life have got to be applied. What great author said man doesn't live on an island, he's surrounded by people? Anything you do reflects and bounces off others. Club life sets a moderate standard. You can do your own thing provided it doesn't interfere with others.

Something else is burning me up too. If I was younger I'd join another club, but I can't. Most clubs are now for teenagers. What about people over twenty-five who won't marry and who need to meet once in a while and have a drink, have a talk somewhere other than a boozer? Where are they? They're probably like me at home watching television. Where's the social contact in that?

I'm not saying that the coffee bars in the West End are evil, but they're tempting. The atmosphere of hot rooms and hot music and loose clothes and drinks and barbiturates conveniently supplied is not a good environment for youngsters, and by youngsters I mean anybody under the age of thirty-five. They are being conditioned, brainwashed. Relationships can't properly develop in artificial hothouses. I insist that it's club life, whether

Jewish or non-Jewish, mixed or not mixed, that makes people more civilized. People who were once on the fringes—the deviants, the kinky ones, the muggers, the sneak thieves—are now part and parcel of the general community. Their proportion is now such that they are affecting the majority. The kids of today are in dire peril. They lack training.

The trouble is you can't force people to do things. They themselves must *want* to return to social life. When their rebellion started, they kicked out some bad ideas but they also kicked out some solid good ones. I'm against the puritanical attitude that children should be seen and not heard, that 'What *I* tell you is right, never mind what *you* think!' But what about taste?—and I don't necessarily mean taste in furniture and clothes which can only come with a cheque book, I mean an appreciation of the finer things such as music and art even though one is not actively involved with them oneself, I mean not coming into a room drunk and ogling and making rude noises, I mean having good table manners and having tolerance and consideration for other people's feelings. And what about security and companionship, the best aspects of family life? A way of life is not the extremes of the high and the low. Children nowadays seem to be only looking at their own side of things. They ask what they are getting, but don't look at what their parents are getting or what they're doing—trying to give them a better life than what *they* had. I remember there was nothing that my mother had or my brothers had or my sister had that I couldn't have. And if they didn't have it they tried to get it for me. I remember all the treats, all the pleasures. I remember Reggie brushing my shoes and combing my hair and taking me to the Workers' Circle in Great Alie Street so that I could hear good songs and music that he knew I'd like. Thus at little cost he gave me an interest and a way of life. Maybe other families are not artistically inclined. But they must have something. They're not animals. They're human beings. If it's not painting or music, it may be just walking along in the country, maybe collecting stamps.

The worst of all evils that corrupt and taint existence is a too early preoccupation with sex. Animals do it. They don't even know they're doing it. It's a normal reaction. They meet the female when she's ready—*he*'s always ready—and Bang! But what about life afterwards? What about companionship? What about a higher and more enduring feeling? You don't feel tired after you've talked to somebody you love. You can talk for hours, you can walk for hours. You can care for them, they can care for you. There's a bond which is physical, but it's mental too, you don't tire of it. Sex you can tire of if you have it for no other reason than it's there. Sex adds a bit of salt to the meat of life, it gives life its flavour. But with too much salt you can go sick or lose the flavour and the taste.

While I was at the Mile End Old Boys', the secretary, Mr Boyd Stanger, Harry's brother, was always a good friend to me and very instrumental in having me enter for competitions. In 1955 he suggested I go in for the AJY Amateur Talent Competition at the Harmony Club in Stamford Hill. There was a rehearsal on the Thursday for the show that was going to take place on the Sunday. When it came for me to do my song, 'Catari', the microphone was working, there was a broad beam of light that didn't affect my eyes, and the pianist was very good. I sang the song and thank you very much. But when I went on the Sunday and it came my turn, all of a sudden the microphone is not even on, I get hit by a spotlight right between the eyes and the pianist is playing the wrong tempo. I sing my song and I go off raging mad. I say to the Stage Manager, 'Why is it you never turned on the mike?' When he told me, 'It must have broken down', I pulled the lead right out and I said, 'Now you've got a permanent problem!' I was fuming. I was choked. I was so upset at this blatant attempt to discredit my performance that I don't even know who won the competition.

It was Boyd Stanger, too, who suggested I join the Old Stepnians' Operatic Society of which he was one of the star performers. The Society met at the Canon Barnett branch of the Stepney Institute. At the Smithy Street branch, I was attending singing classes under the direction of Miss Whitehead who had a nice soprano voice but no real oomph, being typically English and without the emotions essential to a good singer even if they are never fulfilled. Her method was to encourage her better pupils to teach the rest while she accompanied us on the piano.

If you could say that the Mile End Old Boys' was a good solid cake, the Old Stepnians' was the cream and the sugar and the spice and everything that made it nice. It was like the East London Maccabi again, except it had a carefree, abandoned lot of artists whose aims were to sing and to be happy and to put on shows. A lot of the members were single and married women who had belonged for twenty-five years. We met for three hours every Tuesday and in those three hours we had to learn the music and, after a couple of months, the dance routines. Then the scenes were set out and we had a couple of slow and laborious run-throughs before the finished performance when we gave a terrific show on speed. Our object was to raise money for paraplegics and old people and other charities by performing Gilbert and Sullivan operas.

Each production took a year. I joined at a time when they were performing *Ruddigore* for the Toynbee Hall Theatre, so I had to wait until their next production which was *The Gondoliers*, at the Toynbee too. I didn't want to be a principal—acting with words isn't my métier. I was in the chorus. I learned a lot about stage presence, mime-acting and how to manipulate the mouth so as to sing words very, very quickly. Dancing a dance that is very fast while singing a song that is very fast isn't easy!

You hear a lot about theatrical superstitions. Well, when we were doing *The Gondoliers*, for the paraplegics, the first night was fantastic. Nothing went wrong. It was beautiful, right up to standard. At the end of the show everybody was congratulating one another. Harry Stanger, the director and choreographer, was looking very worried. His wife, Ann, our accompanist, was standing beside him. She also was miserable. I said, 'What *is* this?! You didn't do a bad show!' He said, 'Sssh! Tomorrow's going to be terrible!' It was. At the finale of the First Act we were singing 'Farewell gondolieri'. You're supposed to see a gondola being rowed very slowly away by the gondoliers. A very important moment. It stuck right in the middle of the stage, wouldn't move. The director had to crawl behind the scenery and push. Then, during the 'Did you miss me?' quartet in the second half, the mood was interrupted by the clanging of an iron bar. Bang! That was on the Tuesday, and now I know why the Stangers were so miserable—it should have all happened on the Monday!

Same with *The Mikado,* two years later! We were doing it—four nights at the Toynbee and the last at the Scala—for the Golders Green Meals on Wheels, Jewish Section. *The Mikado* is the greatest piece of sustained choral singing that I've ever heard or sung in. It's as near to Grand Opera as makes no difference. The first night was fantastic. Nothing went wrong. Lily Castle sang 'The Moon and I' nicely. Valerie Sass sang Katisha marvellously. I was proud of her. She was a little girl with ginger hair, lovely. Before auditioning, she was worried because she didn't think she had the voice for it. I said, 'Put your chin down a little bit, pick your chest up and think chesty.' She did that, and her voice came out like a magnificent contralto which she developed before the opening night because she was a hard worker. Anyway, I looked at the director afterwards and I thought, 'This is the best show yet and he's miserable. His wife is miserable. His brother, Boyd, is miserable.' I said to Boyd, 'What's the matter? Why is everyone so miserable?' He said, 'It'll be murder tomorrow.' Sure enough, at Katisha's first entrance, when she's trying to denounce Nanki-Poo, she's suddenly singing the part of the chorus and Nanki-Poo is nonplussed and the chorus lost!

Before *The Mikado*, we did *Box and Cox* and *HMS Pinafore* for the Jewish Boy Scouts, Golders Green, at the Rudolf Steiner Hall at the top of Baker Street. One night was a boiler. The girls were flapping their dresses. When I went back to the dressing-room during the interval, one of the principals, who was not in this show because his mother was ill, said very casually, 'Does anybody want any of this iced tea?' I'd never had any iced tea, which I now know is delicious, so, being hot and bothered and sweating like a pig, I accepted, forgetting that with cold tea in a hot stomach you get colic—and I got it for two weeks.

I was always called the one-man tenor line. There were about half a dozen tenors in the chorus. The other five had weak voices, and I had a big one. Something happens to it when I get on stage. I know how to project. There's a scene near the end of the First Act of *The Gondoliers* when all the men are singing 'All hail, O King, whoever you may be!' We happen to be kneeling. My old friend, Manny Fisher, told me that my voice ran right through the theatre with 'All hail, O King!'! In fact, he told me, he heard my voice through the whole production. It wasn't my fault if the other voices had nothing in them and I had some good golden quality.

Our plans were to have the next production, *The Pirates of Penzance*, at the King George's Hall in the Tottenham Court Road. It never happened. We had all the singing prepared, all the dancing. We had invited our guest principals. We were nearly ready. Then, a week before we were supposed to open—and we'd paid nearly £150 for the hall plus costume money and the books, none of which was returned—the D'Oyly Carte came in to London. That killed the production. We pleaded, but they held out on copyright. Our backers lost their gamble, and we were put in the red, cleaned out. It was the end of June, 1965 or '66, just before the summer period of three months when the Institute closed. At the beginning of September, only about a dozen of us returned, and the conductor, Mr Phillips, had resigned. The survivors of the débâcle carried on for about a year doing concerts, mostly for the elderly, but three or four of our principals joined another society which meant the finish.

SIX

For the past fifteen years, quite apart from belonging to, and singing at, the Mile End Old Boys', the Old Stepnians' and Smithy Street, I'd been trying to break into Show Business by every means I knew.

While the tailoring was still dead I thought to myself, 'I'll go round the agencies.' I must have gone to sixteen shabby cubby-holes off the Charing Cross Road and, to some of them, I went two or three times a week, hoping one of them would finally say, 'Let's hear you!' I lied to them. I told them I'd done pub work up North to suggest I'd an experienced background. I said, 'Look, I don't care if you hear me here or in the basement or in the attic, with or without a piano—just hear me sing! If you think I've got possibilities, let me know and let's talk business!' Invariably they said, 'I can't do that, but if you let me know where you're performing I'll come and see you.' I said, 'But I'm *looking* for work! That's why I've come to you!' There was one snide character, I think his name was Jacobs. He dealt with a lot of Irish acts but I went to him as somebody said, 'Being a Yiddisher man, you a Yiddisher boy, maybe . . .' I went with a friend called Adrian I'd met in Westcliffe. He was a good-looking boy and he'd done a couple of years at sea. We go into this fellow Jacobs. I say, 'I'm a singer.' He looks at the handsome boy beside me and says, 'Isn't *he* the singer?' The germ was implanted. Adrian got such a boost out of being mistaken for a singer that he took singing lessons and it finished up that, when I heard him about five years later, he sounded like a gramophone record that had been badly scratched.

The only agency that was of any size or importance was

Bernard Delfont's place just off Oxford Circus near the Underground. I explained to the secretary that I was a singer, I'd been trained and I'd done a bit of club work and I'd like to have an audition, 'if not to be a big star at least to be in the chorus with a chance of going on to sing solo.' Being a Yiddisher girl and feeling for me, she said, 'As a matter of fact Mr Delfont is not in, but his assistant will see you.' He had a chat with me and suggested I try to get into a touring company. Before I went on my way I said, 'I believe in the old saying, "Small company, small time. Big company, big time".' It's a pity I wasn't in on the old pals act. Show Business was a closed shop.

About 1953, I met Danny Samson who had worked himself up to a high position in the Taxi Drivers' Association. He remembered how I sang at the audition for ENSA, and the taxi drivers had this idea that they were going to organize a concert to raise money to give kids a nice day's holiday by the seaside. He said, 'Come along! You'll get through the audition easy. There'll be two dates and if you click with these you're in. You should call yourself "Alex Hartog, the South African Tenor".' He drove me to where they were auditioning on the outskirts of London. Who should be putting on the show but Eddie Bubley who ran the Manhattan Table Tennis Club in Whitechapel and years before had made me an honorary member in return for singing a few songs every two or three weeks in the intervals!

Eddie had a shop in the Lane where he sold dresses and silk underwear. He had been his brother's manager when at nine or ten he appeared in the Music Halls as 'The Little Boy Wonder, Ernie Bubley', playing a violin. He had always kept in touch with this person and that person in show business and sometimes he acted as an agent though when someone once asked him to introduce *me* he said, 'I suggest he puts a placard on his chest with "I Don't Want Any Money, Only Give Me A Chance To Sing" on it and goes into the streets of the West End and sees what happens!'

I sang 'Song of Songs' and got the thumbs up from the committee. Danny was jubilant. So was I. The six chosen acts were standing down near the stage shaking hands and talking when we heard a buzz at the back. Someone on the committee signalled Danny. He went up to them. There was more buzzing.

Danny came back. Bubley had queried the selection and I was out and, out with me, the five other acts.

I didn't see Bubley again for about twenty years. I knew that his agency can't have gone very well because I saw him one Sunday selling dresses and underwear—with scarves as an innovation—on a stall in the Narrow Ways just outside his old shop. It was getting chilly—it was the end of the summer of '73. I said, 'What are you charging for those scarves?' He said, 'No charge to you, tateleh. Tell me which one you want. It's for gornisht (which means for nothing).' 'Blow me!' I said, 'I can pay!' I didn't want him to think I was poverty stricken. He said, 'No, no! just for old time's sake!' I picked out a blue one with the motif of a skier going down a slope. He put it in a bag and said, 'Any time you're passing just give me a nod. You know—keep in touch!' I walked away and I said to myself, 'This lousy scarf is poor compensation for the disappointment you caused me when you could have changed my whole life!!'

But back to the early fifties. The ABC cinemas were using Donald Peers as a cheap means of entertainment, and saying he was looking for a new artist to sponsor and was going to introduce the winning singer on the wireless. What happened was, I went to the Mile End Empire on the Monday and won my heat with 'Hear my song, Violetta'. At the Finals on the Friday the cor blimey who won was a pub singer who stuck his mouth into the microphone and sang a pop song. He brought along about a hundred kids from the district aged twelve, thirteen and fourteen and, after he sang his song, Bang, Bang, Bang! I didn't know that banging was supposed to be applauding. It was between the two of us. For me, clapping, genuine applause. For him, whistling, screaming, banging of feet. The manager picked him as winner. He got ten pounds and I got a complimentary ticket for the month which I tore up in front of him and the audience. I was really upset. My family said I was like a bear with a sore head. Of course at the next show across the water he got slung out because he didn't have his mates with him. My sister-in-law, Milly, said I should have gone to the Regent Cinema, Stamford Hill, which was pro-Jewish.

During the middle fifties, a friend of mine, Alf Gevelb, said why didn't I go to the Finsbury Park Empire and audition for the Carol Levis Show. When I got there, I found his brother, Cyril, had taken over the auditioning as Carol had had a nervous breakdown. I gave my name. I gave my music to the pianist. I sang 'Catari'. In the gallery was a cleaning woman doing a bit of dusting down. When I opened up the voice with 'cori cori grata', that's 'calling, calling for you', she jumped in the air. I petrified Cyril too. He said, 'Oh, yes, we must get in touch with you. Yes, yes, yes.' I haven't heard from him since. But I really made an impact. It wasn't a big theatre, it was a postage stamp stage with a postage stamp auditorium, and I really threw my voice with the help of that microphone—and all my frustration with it!

The next catastrophe was at a Gaumont British or an ABC, way out in the wilds at ten o'clock on a Sunday morning. It took me and two friends about an hour to get there by bus. Now ten o'clock on a Sunday morning I'm not awake, I'm not even living. I wanted to sing 'Che gelida manina' or 'Celeste Aida', both of which give you time to warm up during the song. But no, my friends said, 'Get 'em quick with "La donna è mobile"!' Well, that's all very well when I'm on form, but not first thing in the morning. When I went on the stage and sang 'La donna è mobile' I wasn't even warmed up when I'd finished. A bass-baritone with a nothing-unusual voice is winner. A couple of Irish tenors are protesting and I'm protesting. The competition was called 'The Mario Lanza Competition'. They were supposed to be looking for a tenor?

As a matter of fact Mario Lanza was the cause of a dispute in a restaurant I used to go to called 'Jack's' on the corner of Commercial Road and Christian Street. I was sitting in Jack's one evening and up comes the name of Mario Lanza. I say he's a fraud. I let go with enough to get me ten years in the nick. I say, 'He's not a tenor. He can't act. He shouts. He screams. He whines. He drawls the words, he mimes them, he eats them and spits them out. When is he going to sing?' That was on the one night. The following night I come along and Jack who has enjoyed my tirade has a friend of his there called Joe Jacobs who was fight manager before the war for a few of the East End boys such as Harry Lazarus, Alec Phillips and Sid Nathan. I wasn't to know Joe had just come out of hospital after recovering from a coronary thrombosis. Anyhow, as soon as he mentions Mario Lanza favourably I don't have a go at Mario Lanza, I have a go at Jack and Joe. I ask them are they trying to insult me. I tell them that to bait a person on purpose shows they haven't the intelligence of arses. That was on Wednesday. I came in on the Thursday and Jack's wife said, 'I suppose you know that Mr Jacobs died in the night?' I felt bad. I've a good command of English and I'd torn Jack and Joe to pieces with words. I don't like mickey-takers. Their sense of superiority reveals *their* inferiority. It's only people with inferior minds who try to lower somebody else or make him feel inadequate or leave him standing out on a verbal limb to give themselves a kick. Joe's death didn't have anything to do with me, but I didn't like to think that the last remaining hours of his life were burdened with my attack on his mental powers.

To continue with my Show Business efforts. In 1955 I came out of Johnnie Isaacs' fish and chip shop in Whitechapel with Jack Conway and demonstrated to him a couple of times how to take the B Flat in 'O Paradiso'. Jack Conway was a tenor in the Mile End Old Boys' and the only pupil I've ever had. He did everything wrong, he sang as though someone had his two hands around his throat and was trying to choke him. But somehow the natural voice broke always through. Because he showed good taste—in other words because he appreciated the way I sang—I taught him, as I had been taught, how to relax the throat, also about the half smile, pitching, breathing, diction and phrasing, all those things that are the armoury of a singer. In two months his voice so improved that he left his job with an insurance firm and applied for an audition with a company going on tour with *The Desert Song*. They accepted him for the chorus and he went on tour for three or four months and afterwards got another chorus part, this time in *The Student Prince*. I received from him fourteen or fifteen letters in which he confirmed that the advice I had given him was very beneficial and that the small principals and the people in the chorus agreed. He always addressed me on the envelopes as 'Alex Hartog (Tenor)'. In the end he got married and went back to Insurance but at least he had beaten the system, smashed his way into Show Business and made the grade to a certain extent. Well, I was demonstrating how to take this B Flat in the 'O Paradiso' outside Johnnie Isaacs' and who should be hearing it on the next floor above but Johnnie Isaacs' daughter who admired the magic of the sound. I went in again the next night or the night after and she said, 'I didn't know you could sing like that! Why don't you make a recording because I know a person who, if you impress him with your voice on a record, could do something for you? He knows a lot of people in Show Business and he's the manager of a music shop in New Oxford Street.' I rang up HMV in Oxford Street so that I could make a record to take to this potential do-gooder, and found out that a session would cost me thirty shillings. As I was on a three and a half day week I was able to arrange to be at the studio next morning at half past ten.

About half past nine I got on a bus, thinking I'd be there by ten. Didn't get there till ten to eleven—there was a conspiracy, today was Bottleneck Day, there was a hold up in the traffic from Whitechapel right through. Finally I got off the bus between stops and walked the last hundred yards. 'Oh, you should have been here at half past ten. But we *can* fit you in. I'm sorry but our regular pianist is away ill, but the reserve is all right.' She wasn't. Maybe the big occasion frightened her or something because, and I know I shouldn't be hard as it was a first time for me as well as her, she had forgotten everything she ever learned. She made me very worried. All my singing life it's been a struggle to find decent pianists and when I've found them I've lost them. I've always said that if I could have found a decent pianist early on in my life I might have made a go of my career.

We started off on a good note. The recording manager had a sour face because I was late, and I was narked because I didn't have the regular pianist and I was wondering what the hell she was going to do. She was nineteen or twenty, typically English and well meaning, and if she'd ever had any technique she'd left it in bed when she got out of it. Lookswise you could walk her by in the street and not feel you'd missed anything. He was about thirty-two, my own age, about six foot one and skinny with a small moustache and dressed in a navy blue suit. He immediately showed his ignorance or sense of superiority or both by not bothering to find out the type of voice I had in advance of his technical preparations.

It was a large room about twenty-five feet by twenty-five, the same height also. It was supposed to be a perfect cube. I had decided to sing Toselli's 'Serenata'—'Like a golden dream in my heart ever biding'—and the 'O Paradiso' ('Mi batte il cor') from Meyerbeer's opera, *L'Africana*. There's a story that Meyerbeer's real name was Beer. His uncle, called Meyer, who was a very wealthy man, said he would leave him his money if he joined the name Meyer to his as he didn't have any children. Or was it the other way round?

The girl ran rather trippily over the music, and the snotty-nosed recording manager stuck the microphone—on a boom—about three feet away from my face and about a foot above my head which was wrong because it made me raise my chin. He then went into his kiosk which had a small control panel. I asked to sing the 'O Paradiso' first. He must have been a bit of a sadist because I sang the whole of it before he decided it wasn't three feet away he wanted the microphone, it was four and a half. And I'm still looking up. I don't like that. The microphone should be level with my mouth. So I sang it again, with the boom five feet away. Again—six feet away. The whole thing! After six times singing right through, the microphone must have been over twenty feet away. It was nearer to the other wall than me. And it was still higher than my head. And we still hadn't recorded. And the pianist was still murdering the introduction, giving me no tempo, no dramatic quality, no build-up. The seventh version was the version he recorded. I wasn't to know that he was rounding it out and that as soon as the needle approached danger point he was shutting down volume. Why didn't he say in the first place, 'Don't sing big because I can pick you up and I can control the volume.' He must have been the reserve recorder just as the girl was the reserve pianist.

The boom was still over near the far wall and I said that for a contrast I'd sing Toselli's 'Serenata' softly. I told the pianist that I'd like it done a little quicker than what was in the music to give it a lilt, but she went on with her plodding act. A good pianist is oh so important to a singer! If he's caught a mood she should work with him. I was once invited to sing at the King George's Hall, Stepney, and this bloody stupid cow was killing me with her accompaniment. The difference between a pianist and an accompanist is that a pianist plays the music *his* way with *his* interpretation, but an accompanist lets the singer take the lead and just follows and embroiders. It's a duet. Now this girl was doing her best with the 'Serenata' but, let's face it, she was inadequate and should never have been allowed in the studio.

I was singing very softly. I was like as if I was crooning to a baby. When I finished he said, '*That*'s the volume I wanted you to sing!' Then he played the 'O Paradiso' back to me. It sounded like old boots and gravy. I said, 'What have you done? Where are the highlights? Where are the runs to the B Flat?' He said, 'The voice was too big.' I said, 'Do you mean to say that when I was opening up you were shutting down?! You've rounded me off! I sound like a baritone. Where's my top notes? Where's my range? I want to see your manager! What is this?! I've got an incompetent pianist and I've got an arrogant and incompetent recorder who forgets to tell me I can sing softly and he'll still pick up my voice, and I've knocked myself out seven times singing the lousy old "O Paradiso" and he kills it!' I was so horrified and I got him so mixed up that he forgot to play the 'Serenata'. He said, 'Maybe I can correct them with another recording. I'll do my best to eradicate the mistakes, though it will cost you ten bob more for the extra shell.'

But by trying to pick the 'O Paradiso' up from the brown boots stage with more treble, he may have made the voice lighter and purer and more heady but he also took the manhood out of it—and he couldn't put back the top notes he'd whipped off, either.

Not only did he give me a second 'O Paradiso', he was so farmisht that he tried to console me with another version of the 'Serenata' as well. He lightened *that* up when there was no need to! So I like the first 'Serenata' best and I don't like either one of the 'O Paradiso's' and I couldn't afford another recording. My feelings at the time were so intense that only sheer violence would have done them justice.

I explained the position to Miss Isaacs and she told me to

go anyway to this friend of hers and gave me his address in New Oxford Street. The only remark he made on hearing me was, 'That pianist wasn't good!' He was obviously only pretending to show interest for Miss Isaacs' sake. To get out you don't have to be told to get out and you don't have to be thrown out. I never spoke to Miss Isaacs again. I had performed a feat of strength to no avail. I was drained of energy. The ground was swept from under me. I nearly gave up trying for want of encouragement. The spirits were continuing to have a game at my expense.

Three years later, though, I well and truly defeated them—or else they were on my side. For once, I came up trumps.

I bowled along as usual one Friday night to Miss Whitehead's singing class at Smithy Street, where my friend Frank Weiner, an outstanding bass-baritone who, if he'd had any luck and been born in another country would have been recognized, said, 'Did you see the *East London Advertiser* this week?' I said, 'Why?' He said, 'There's to be a competition between Stepney and Poplar at the Poplar Civic. Six or seven turns from each of the boroughs are to be judged by a panel of Entertainment Officers from the Butlin Camps. Why don't we enter?' I said, 'OK. Where are they having the auditions?' He said, 'The Mile End Empire this Sunday from ten o'clock onwards.' I said, 'Right! I'll meet you outside about eleven.'

Come the Sunday we went in to the Mile End Empire. Probably two hundred people were there to audition, as well as friends to gee them up. It was a pretty packed place. The spotlights were on, so you couldn't see far into the auditorium once you got onto the stage. Four or five people were sitting down in the first row, and one of them would get up and say, 'Thank you very much' or 'Will you give your name and address to so and so (the man who was standing in the wings)'. If you had to give your name and address to the man standing in the wings, that meant you were being considered. If he said, 'Thank you very much', that was it. We were all sitting down and going seat by seat according to who was nearest to the stage. You were pointed to and you got up and you gave your music and you performed.

Let's get my friend Frank into his true perspective. He's

either a concert or an opera singer. He's not a microphone singer, and they had a microphone. All concert and opera singers sing from strength and know how to control their voices. A microphone only throws them out, it makes their voices bigger than they want. They don't know the power that's in it and the sound-men, without them knowing, can turn it up and make their voices blarey. As I learned in the recording studio, you've got to back away and croon, and if you've got a big voice you've lost your main asset. In fact, a person who has always sung from strength and then has to use a microphone will find within a couple of months that he's lost his idea of projection, of the balance which is powerful but not too shouty, of how to modulate, how to bring out and how to coax. Anyway, Frank sings, 'Your philandering days are over' from *Don Giovanni*. It's a very light thing but he couldn't use the microphone and they didn't like him, they say, 'Thank you very much'. And to me he's a good singer. I thought, 'Oh, help!'

I'm next. I will say one thing for them. They didn't just do what the so-called experts do in pro-circles. You stand up and start singing. 'Thank you very much. Do you know anything else?' They hear that for about half a minute, don't give you a chance to warm up and show you've got something. Then they say, 'Thank you very much. Don't call us, we'll call you. And the next, please!' No, they let me sing Leoncavallo's 'La Mattinata' right through and then 'Nessun' dorma' from *Turandot*, Puccini's last opera. Now what made me sing 'Nessun' dorma' when I could have sung a ballad, I don't know. 'Nessun' dorma' is not for openers, and I did something I'd never done before and I've never done afterwards—I gave the throat a bit of a strain. I had a bit of a head cold and the mucus went into the throat. The man said, 'Thank you very much', then 'Just hang on a moment!' and disappeared into the darkness at the back. Whatever somebody said to him—was it an LCC official who had heard me sing at one of the three consecutive Annual Dinners of the Stepney Institute at the Three Nuns?—he returned and told me to give my name and address to the man in the wings. I commiserated with Frank and, in about a week's time, received a letter from the Mayor's office asking me would I please turn up for the Stepney run-through in front of an audience of between three and four thousand people at the Troxy next Saturday before the last picture.

The Stepney team had a coloured man in it, about forty-five, not handsome but cheerful and with a bass-baritone which he could modulate for folk songs at the microphone. There was also a girl of twenty-four or twenty-five who, though she didn't have the power, wouldn't use the microphone enough. There was Johnnie, an Irish boy with a light voice, who sang popular ballads. There were two semi-professional middle-aged chaps with a Flanagan and Allen act they performed in public houses. There was a raucous pop group that wore mohair suits which changed from dark brown into gold according to the lights. There was also the Brady Boys' Choir and myself. I was all dressed up in my tuxedo and white handkerchief, sitting behind the screen with the rest and waiting to sing 'M'appari tutt'-amor' in Italian and the 'Mattinata' in English, though, unfortunately, through giving my throat that bit of a strain at the audition, I'd developed a relaxed larynx. With us were two people from the Mayor's office, a passable pianist and a man to suggest the order.

First on were the Brady Boys. They didn't go down too well. Their conductor, Grenville Jenner, couldn't control them. Maybe in their own atmosphere in the Brady Club surrounded by friends they did well, but in the harsh world of trying to entertain people who don't know you and don't particularly want to know you they were overawed and only got by. The girl sang her couple of songs. She needed to use the microphone more. The Negro was good. The two old-timers sang, danced, cracked jokes. The light Irish tenor sang a couple of popular ballads. Then there was me, and we finished up with the pop group. For one of their numbers the leader took off a Jerry Colonna number, but a bit too near the microphone.

As I waited in the wings . . . Here comes the old cliché about the mind going back! But this time it went all the way!—I was a little boy again of three and a half, who walked out of the Stroud House, Bermondsey, one Sunday evening, and saw people queuing to go into the building opposite. I asked a young fellow at the door, 'What's on?', thinking it was a picture house. He said, 'The Church Club's putting on a concert.' I asked,

'How much?' He looked down at me. 'For children, a penny.' I paid a penny, and I'd to go up two flights of stairs to a large hall, and I chose a seat on the left of the aisle, about two rows back. I saw sketches—there was one about a ghost who pretended to be a human-being. I heard Music Hall choruses, popular songs . . . I was entranced. It was my first taste of Show Business. It was my first Variety Show. It was my baptism of fire. I went every night for the whole week! They used to greet me at the door. 'Hello! That boy's here again!' But I still had to pay a penny every time! The next show I saw was the last season of the London Music Hall, Shoreditch. My brother, Alan, took me. I laughed at Max Miller's jokes though I was only four!

Tonight was *my* turn to be on a Variety Bill of some importance. And what an evening it was! My voice was at full blast, and at full blast they used to say at the Mile End Old Boys' you could get up off your seat, walk out of the hall, out of the building, across the road and fifty yards down to the bus stop and still hear me. I stood two to three feet away from the microphone and began with the 'M'appari tutt'amor', which was a mistake. It begins soft and you've even got to go up to a G soft and I forgot my relaxed vocal cords. When I got to that G, there was the true note and a ghost of a note with it. I heard somebody laugh, but I carried on and got fair applause. Then I sang the 'Mattinata' and took no chances with the soft notes. I sang happy and big. The voice was ringing. I felt the audience thaw like a loving woman. They stood up to applaud, and when they stood up to applaud you at the Troxy you knew you'd done something. It never seemed to end. They'd to bring on the pop group to quieten everybody down. After bowing five or six times in gratitude, I was looking left and right to find an empty space to walk through among the well-wishers who were crowding both the wings. A stage hand gave me the thumbs-up. He'd heard me from the flies. He said, 'I always like to hear them from the flies. If they're good they're good, and if they're bad they're terrible, and you were good, kid!'

Another week to go before the competition at the Poplar Civic! I was worried. I was trying the soft notes and I could still hear the ghost. I'd never strained my voice before in all my years of singing. But now for the change that comes over me when the big occasion takes place! I've been known to be exhausted from work, to have a sore throat, a headache, but give me the occasion and I forget all of them, I suspend them and, for that ten minutes or quarter of an hour, I'm the singer I want to be, and then I relapse into the cold or headache or I feel tired again.

On the Saturday, both teams meet round two o'clock to rehearse with the organist. They take Poplar first. I'm looking at the opposition. About three or four of their acts are miming to records, phoney artists who use the talent of others for their own lack of it. I've a contempt for miming so I walk away. They go off-stage and we come on. I see everybody perform. We go round the corner for a cup of tea five-ish, come back six-ish to make up for the show at seven. My rehearsal hasn't gone too well—the mucus was still there; I was even clearing my throat while singing. The compère didn't seem impressed.

In the dressing-room I'm doing my diaphragm exercises. Then I begin to open up singing—big notes, big powerful chesty notes. Tonight I'm going to prove myself. The sound is bouncing off the walls and ceiling and everybody's looking.

The officials tossed a coin and Poplar went on first. Behind the stage was an enormous table laden with cold drinks, and plates and plates of sandwiches. Because we lost the toss and went on second, Poplar after their show were able to go backstage and nosh all the grub so that when we came back we got nothing.

I watched their show from the back of the Gallery. Except for the Brady Boys' Choir who were somewhere else having tantrums, our team was sat together in a group. The coloured fellow was sipping from a flask to give himself Dutch courage. There's very few of us who have the calm nerve to face an audience hot, cold or indifferent. I've seen a girl with a lovely voice look down at the people and freeze. The words didn't come out of her mouth. She lifted up her head and sang beautifully for a minute. Then she glanced down and she froze again. An audience can frighten. But I've worked out a theory, I've cancelled out this business of nerves. I asked myself once, 'Tell me, does being nervous help you?' I said, 'No!' and because I knew Alex all my life and I realized he meant well, I was never nervous again, I took his advice. Now, I'm sitting there at the back of the Gallery and I'm hearing Poplar's first two acts—two young girls miming and after them a chap who's miming—and then I'm sleeping! I don't know if I snored and gave the game away, but all of a sudden the shorter of the semi-professionals who were to do the Flanagan and Allen, he gave me a bit of a shake and said, 'What do you think of our chances?' I said, 'Are you joking?! We'll beat them easy! They're all rubbish!'

Now when we went down round the back at the interval I had the sense, the feeling that, apart from this man and his partner, and apart from the coloured man with his cheer from the gin or whatever, the others were petrified. It frightens some people just to sit or stand around and wait, and they'd been sitting for more than an hour while I snored. So I decided to take them in charge, turn our team into a self-admiration society. I was so busy patting everybody on the back and pepping them up and telling them how to go on, that I missed hearing the Brady Boys again! I said, 'Look! You can beat this lot. They're nothing!' I said to the girl, 'Pardon me, my dear, but you've got a lovely voice. Don't hide it from the public. When you stand out there in front of that microphone, get within six or eight inches. Let them hear you! They'll want to hear you!' To Johnnie I said, 'You've got the same problem. You've got a lovely voice but it's not big enough, so come close to that microphone!' Then I told the leader of the group, 'When you take off Jerry Colonna, don't blare. Your voice is big enough. It's as big as mine. Don't worry, kid. Don't let the nerves get you. You've got nothing to beat here!' I cheered them up. They relaxed, and Stepney won by a landslide.

I was fifth on the bill. With the first note that came out of my mouth I thought I would knock that microphone off the stage, but it was a Gigli type of head note, soft and gentle. I said to myself right away, 'That's good, boy! That's good! Let it just go for a while!' I went through the first few lines and then I warmed it up a bit, but not too much. Then suddenly something happened. It had happened before at the club but never in front of an audience I didn't know. What a pity my mother had been passed away six or seven months and couldn't hear me! They'd have killed you if you dropped a pin in there! They didn't stop clapping for five minutes after I'd sung that aria. The eight hundred or so on the ground level were standing up. Now I sang the 'Mattinata'. I was really alight, fighting mad, maybe because I'd spoilt the run-through and the worst critic of me is me and I brood on it. I said to myself, 'Why don't you open up a bit?' and I did, and it took five minutes before the last act could go on. All the compère could say as I finally went off was, 'Well! . . . *Well*!'

About two weeks afterwards, I received a letter of commendation from the Mayor, thanking me for my efforts. He asked would I care to take part in a follow-up competition at the Poplar Civic between Stepney and Bow. I thanked him for his praise but refused his invitation on the grounds that the catering arrangements at the last concert were poor to say the least. They took well over £100 in ticket sales and paid out about a fiver on the sandwiches and lemonade which the Poplar team ate up in the interval. I hadn't had anything to eat since two, and I couldn't eat until past eleven o'clock when I got home.

I'd another singing experience worth a mention, but it wasn't the most satisfying as there wasn't any competition.

One Friday in 1962 I went along to the Smithy Street and I was called down to the office where Miss Murphy, the Assistant Principal, explained that Smithy Street were going to send a team of singers and musicians to the Stratford and East London Music Festival. One or two pianists and violinists and a string quartet were going to do their thing, and myself and Frank Weiner were to represent the singers. Frank and I worked out that I would do an operatic aria—'Celeste Aida'—and that we'd do together H. Lane Wilson's 'Tenor and Baritone Duet'. He would also sing 'Even the bravest hearts' from *Faust* in the Baritone Section and something from Verdi's *Requiem* in the Oratorio.

The Festival began off on a Monday evening. We bowled over to the Stratford Town Hall about six o'clock and waited till about eight when the duets came on. There were only about five or six pairs. Two young girls who sang a Mozart duet went by unnoticed by me. Frank and I got up and sang the 'Tenor and Baritone'. As a matter of fact in those days I was hoping to work up some sort of an act with Frank, piecing together our two voices in duets like the 'Tenor and Baritone', 'The Beaux Gendarmes', 'On the threshold of the Temple' from *The Pearl Fishers,* and also doing some solo items. I was always trying! To get back to the main theme—the duettists that went before us at the Festival were non-eventers, all with small voices and, as I said, the two young girls with their Mozart didn't register. The adjudicator was Mr Harold Noble. After praising the brilliant, full, mature voices of the tenor and the baritone, he awarded Frank and me less points than the two little girls and gave them First Place and us Second. Though the 'Tenor and Baritone' is a good test for singing, it isn't opera, and Mr Noble was an opera snob. Yet a middle-aged woman came up to us afterwards and asked would we care to join her operatic society in Stratford, and we just had to refuse as we had prior commitments with the Smithy Street and the Old Stepnians'. Then the mother of the two little girls came up, very, very embarrassed. She said, 'They keep on appearing in concerts with this Mr Noble and he keeps on giving them First Place!' What's more, they never showed at the Final Concert on the Saturday.

On the Tuesday, Frank with his amazing voice—the deep power of a bass combined with the lyrical quality of a baritone—cantered away with 'Even the bravest hearts', and, on the Thursday, though he sang gloriously, he was beaten by about a point because the *Requiem* wasn't considered to be Oratorio. He should have sung something from Handel's *Messiah.*

On the Wednesday I sang 'Celeste Aida'. There is a problem with the stage at the Stratford Town Hall. If you stand more than a foot away from the edge of the stage you can hardly hear your own voice so, as all I could hear was a whisper, I kept saying to myself, 'Alex, more voice! More voice!' I was over-projecting. I won just the same. I suppose all the competitors suffered from the same handicap. The Adjudicator's Report said, 'The voice is right for Radames. Resonant and operatic in proportions. In the aria itself soften the high F's a little. Make it more *tender* in the main.' I would have, if I could have heard myself! 'Fine ringing high B flats. The singing is well in the rôle's traditional portrayal. Scale down the *parlando.*' I felt pleased I'd won, as it was an open competition. But—and maybe

I'm speaking from a sense of superiority, I don't know—I never heard anybody in my section that remotely approached me.

At the Final Concert on the Saturday night, instead of being given an old-fashioned enormous silver cup, I was given a modern thing like a large teacup. I was told it was going to be sent to the silversmith's across the road and that in a couple of days I could call and collect it and hold it for a year. But the spirits were working overtime. When I called about two weeks later, the silversmith's said the cup had gone back to the organizers. I tried to find the organizers through the porter at the Town Hall, but they'd disappeared up in a cloud of smoke as they always do until about two weeks before the next Festival. So, somewhere, there is a silver cup with my name saying I won the Opera Solo Singing at Stratford in 1962, though I never held it for more than about two seconds.

SEVEN

My mother died on a Friday morning early in February, 1958. It's supposed to be very lucky when a Jewish person dies on a Friday morning just before Sabbath, but I'll always resent the *way* she died. Churchill was in danger of dying at the same time. He pulled through because he had all the best medical attention, and she died with the colic in agony. I looked after her, so did nurse companions from the Bikur Cholim, for near on two years. Then, at one o'clock on the Saturday of her last week, I went to Woolworth's to get some pressed beef. She was sitting in the big armchair covered with two or three blankets. I was away for half an hour. When I returned, she was lying on the floor and the armchair was on its side and the blankets strewn on the floor. The moisture of a cold was coming from her nose. I immediately ran around to Dr Chazan's surgery in Toynbee Street, and he had her taken in an ambulance to Bancroft Road Hospital. By now she was in a coma. I travelled with her. The sister of the ward gave me a card saying I could sit with her morning, afternoon, evening, any time and as long as I liked. Betty and all my brothers and sisters-in-law came at intervals to see her during the week. On the Wednesday evening, my eldest brother, Morry, told me in all seriousness that the doctor had told him that he did not expect my mother to survive the week. I went on the Thursday evening and sat with her from about seven o'clock until nine, and when the nurse came round to make up her bed she never wanted me to go. I said, 'Mum, I'm going out for a moment and I'll be back when she's made your bed', and to seal it I put my cap into her hands and she seemed satisfied. I came back and stayed with her until the nurses changed and the other patients were putting out their lights. I promised I'd be back to see her next day as soon as I finished work. It was a tremendous shock when, at seven o'clock next morning, a policeman knocked to notify me with a slip of paper that she'd passed away during the night.

I phoned my brothers. They all came down. We started getting the medical and the death certificates at about half past eight and we never finished until half past twelve. We decided to sit shivah in the 18, Carter House. During the four hours it took us to do the business, my sister-in-law, Kitty, Steve's wife, put her big mouth in and decided that we should sit at *her* place in the Stamford Hill. Then she had a row with me because I went out for a bite to eat and was back a bit later than two when we were supposed to leave for the Burial Ground. The upshoot of it was that my sister, Betty, sat shivah with me at Carter House while everybody else went up to Stamford Hill where Steve and Kitty lived. Betty got permission from her husband to leave her kids with him, and came to me about eight o'clock on the Sunday. Because members of the family can't go out for a week, friends and neighbours are supposed to come round with gifts of cake and food and to wish you a long life and talk to you, cheer you up, no misery. Not a dicky bird! Milly, who sold socks and stockings on a stall near to Alan who had taken over my mother's stall twenty years before, knocked on the door on the Monday afternoon and said to me, through the letter-box, 'Where's everybody?' When I told her the rest of the family were sitting shivah up in the Stamford Hill, she said she'd go up there. You're not allowed to cook but you've got to survive, so Betty and I were going out to a restaurant to eat and coming back and sitting on our own. That week really dragged.

From then on I was alone and vulnerable. Everything had suddenly turned off and no one was coming to see me. Within a few days I met a friend I'd known since schooldays. I'll call him Jerry. To me he looked on the floor and I needed company so for five months he slept on the couch in my sitting-room and that couch was very comfortable. I gave him a couple of blankets and there was always plenty of grub in the larder. I tell you, he could have stayed there for ten years, eating and sleeping, no cost. Just the fact that he was company was enough for me. So Jerry said to himself, 'Here's an easy mark. Let's take him!' He told me a business about how he could arrange a deal that for a hundred pounds' worth of salmon he could earn me six pounds profit a time, and we could do it two or three times every week. I got involved. Before I knew what had happened, he took away from me a hundred pounds in savings, the sixty pounds I received under my mother's will and about £150 from a Life Insurance Policy I cashed in in advance. No business agreement—friend's word and all that. I lost every penny. For five years he spun me a Fanny and for five years I'd to keep on his good side because I hoped to get back what I lent him. My brother, Reggie, wanted me to press charges. Jerry would have gone to prison. But him going to prison wasn't going to get me my money back. I decided this was not for me. I couldn't afford that type of justice. I was hoping he'd have a pang of conscience.

What motivates a man like Jerry, a man who will con people not that he sees once a week, or once a month, but with whom he's living side by side? Is it greed? Is it evil just for the sake of doing evil? Many times he said to me, 'Let's shake hands on it because our word means everything to us.' He betrayed his word. A thief who doesn't know you, he has to have a certain amount of courage. He sneaks in, takes what he wants and there's nothing personal. OK! Mazel tov! But when a man comes into your life, into your home, sees the good, bad and indifferent things and takes whatever you've got of value, he's the dirtiest rat that infests civilization.

Till then I had done my share. If somebody needed a few bob, a cup of tea, a cheese roll, a few words—just the ordinary human consideration of one person for another—I gave it to him. And now all that was turned against me. Jerry took me for a fool. And I wasn't a fool. Lionel, another friend of mine, cast a slur on my intelligence. He said, 'How could you be taken in?' I said, 'If you went to school with somebody, grew up with him, knew his family, mixed with them after the war, in short if he was a friend of yours for thirty odd years, would you disbelieve him when he said he could help you do a little business?' I introduced him to Jerry with his fresh complexion, moustache and happy, good-looking face, and he said to me afterwards, 'It is possible to be taken in by him.'

Jerry whipped away my capital. It took me four, five, six years to save most of that money, a pound a week, thirty bob a week. I'd gone without. I used to say to my friends when things got a bit slack and I was out of work, 'It's a good job I've got a few hundred pounds put by because it gives me a sense of security and independence.' Jerry not only took away my money, he also took away my faith in human nature. I'm not the gullible, open-handed, open-minded person I was. He destroyed that part of me which was pure good. I still like people but my trust is limited and, as regards to money, I'm a tightwad. It's only my sister I'd help. I weigh up everybody else. We get along provided they don't expect me to lend them any money or invest. But as soon as they start talking business, I freeze because I remember. I'd rather give than run the risk of having to ask for something back that belonged to me in the first place.

When I gave up asking Jerry to give me back my money, I tried to get it back in other ways. He took from me my three hundred odd pounds and turned me into a gambler for ten years which cost me thousands. Like any working person I did the Pools and I liked to have a week-end bet on the horses—a single or a double. Now I tried to win back what I'd lost in the gambling clubs, and the more I won the more I gambled and the more I lost again. It was a vicious circle. It's so easy for people to say it was my own fault and that I could have stopped sooner. But could I? Wasn't I the victim of circumstances and environment and the spirits using me to write their story?

There are some people who gamble because they are frustrated in their ambitions and they have a subconscious desire to kill themselves or to bankrupt themselves. Others are on their own and the only time they can get any company or any pleasure is in a crowded room where there are what they call—it's funny but it's true—their 'fellow sufferers'. I belonged to both categories, and I was as dependent on gambling as a drunkard is dependent on alcohol.

A gambler will gamble on anything—the turn of a card, which of two flies on a wall will be the first to fly off. Maybe there's horses in the afternoon, or greyhounds. He just has to spend a couple of minutes reading a newspaper and he'll play, win or lose. He doesn't care if he loses. There's no value to the money in his pocket, it's only for the purposes of gambling. He's all wrapped up in this thing which is a disease. I've been through it. I was advised by so many well-wishers and friends and relations. They all said very solemnly, 'Ooh, you'll want to stop gambling like this! It'll take you down to the gutter and below! You'll finish up as nothing! And *with* nothing! You won't have a suit of clothes on your back. You're working for the bookmakers!' 'Working for the bookmakers' appealed to my Jewish heart. I don't like bookmakers. Bookmakers are the gambler's enemy. But I didn't take any notice. People talking will not affect the thing. It is only you, you personally. *You* must make the decision and it's not easy. Smoking, gambling, drinking, these things aren't stopped with a flick of the fingers. You've got to find a mental process whereby you can retract from what you were doing before, so it becomes less and less and less and less until finally you reduce it to a bare minimum and, even then, you've got to be carefully on your guard because at a time of stress you can slip right back in the hopes that some craving or some unhappiness will be forgotten.

Albos's was the name of a gambling place I used to go to in Little Somerset Street long before I took up gambling. People gambled there on three-red snooker, the short sprint. The game could be over in five or ten minutes. Players put anything from five shillings to a pound on their own game. The champions even put on two, three, four pounds, and mobs of heavy boys bet on their man and small punters bet among themselves. There was a short, tubby man who used to have a couple of elastic bands on the hand he rested on the table so as to keep the bridge firm. Though his opponent might be a consistently good player, he himself never lost more games than what he won. It was a tradition that towards the end of the evening, when his opponent was flagging, after four to five or even six hours of constant play, he would run out a winner in the last two or three games. So he was called 'Meal Ticket'—and with good cause. Another player was called The Kid. One evening The Kid was playing an electrician from over the water in front of a crowd of about three hundred. The Kid was a fantastic player, good-looking, curly black hair, always dressed smart, you could almost say he was a hustler. But he had horn-rimmed glasses and tonight, out of vanity, he took them off. He could hardly see for the first few games. Meal Ticket, realizing what was happening, walked over very quietly and said, 'Shmuck!'—a penis may be beautiful and attractive and dual purpose, but it hasn't got a brain and The Kid wasn't doing any thinking—'You're playing for other people's money! You're a professional player and all these people are backing you. What have you got to be so proud about? Be proud when you beat this man fifty times out of fifty! Be proud when you give these people back the money they've lost on you on three games already!' Such wisdom appealed to The Kid and he put on his horn-rimmed glasses and he toused the life out of this man who'd come from South London.

There was also two-handed rummy. No money was supposed to be shown. In those days gambling wasn't so easy. We had a runner called Phil for the horses. He sat on a chair waiting, and, as soon as he got three or four people who wanted a bet, he'd phone the bookmakers. Then he'd go away for about half an hour and pay in all the money which he'd taken, and pull back any winnings and pay you back the same evening.

Pity that Albos's is now down. People could go there to gamble but, if they didn't want to gamble, they could sit down and have a cup of tea and a cake or a sandwich and talk to their friends. I used to go there on a Friday night. I used to ignore the cards and I never backed the snooker players. I used to go to the canteen after singing at the Smithy Street, have a cup of tea and a cake and sit down and wait for Lennie, a violinist friend from the Mile End Old Boys' or, if he was there already, we'd have a cup of tea together, 'How are you getting on?', talk about work, nothing in my mind about gambling. Then when a table was empty we'd get up, play a couple of games for half an hour, which only cost us a shilling each, then have a rest and maybe go back for a bit more snooker later.

Albos's was a very friendly type of place, a simple set-up, a social club, a gathering of Jews. It opened at four or five in the evening and closed at six or seven in the morning, and a barber was in attendance every day of the week. On the Sunday, the pre-war East End Jews who'd made it good used to come back on a sentimental journey from Golders Green, Stamford Hill, Southend, Brighton . . . These were the cream, the old villains talking over the old glories. During the week, the members were mostly traders off the barrows, and small time crooks. In fact, before the repeal of the Gaming Acts, the police could have closed the place and nicked practically everybody there! They knew that these people had money in their pockets and that a halfpenny in front of a player could mean ten bob or a pound or two pound, and you weren't supposed in them days to play even with a halfpenny. But they made sure the place stayed open so as to keep an eye on the little villains of the district. They encouraged the Boss not to bar them, and, for a return, one of the housemen—the nark—would inform if there was anybody flashing any money or jewellery or dressing in new clothes or wearing a watch or smoking a cigar, and the police would get it down in their book. They knew what to associate it with—a shop raid, say—and they'd wait till he was away from the club and then the car would pull up.

But there were no real villains, no hard men, at Albos's—or The Spieler as we used to call it. Mind you, there was a lot of the Run-Out Merchants, not to mention the Find the Lady and the Crown and Anchor mobs. The Find the Lady mob have three cards—two aces and a queen. They shuffle them around and a person has to guess where the queen is. They let what they call the 'gee' win a few times to give you confidence but, once you start putting money on yourself, they take it. The game is fixed. They can feint and move so quick with the hands that they deceive the eye. The Crown and Anchor mob run a form of fixed bingo in the Kursaals at the seaside. They've got their own gee-men who will have the winning lines and win the big prizes and let the mug-punters win the small ones. The street Run-Out Merchants start by giving things away. 'Here, lady, have this pen! Here, gentleman, don't say you bought this diary, say you found it or pinched it!' They're drawing everybody in. Now they're getting a crowd around them. They come out with, 'Will you give me a pound, Madam, for this box of cutlery?' She's one of the gees in the crowd and says, 'Yes.'

'Well, I'm not going to charge you a pound, it's yours for two and six.' So he gives her this box of cutlery for two and six. It's all cheap made and bought from a special warehouse. Uri Geller's supposed to bend things. These things bend of themselves, not to mention the silver plating coming away with the first wash. It's cheap rubbish that looks terrific in the box and the most expensive thing is the velvet they've put into it—that must cost about a halfpenny a yard! 'Will you give me half a quid for this?' 'Yes.' 'I don't want half a quid. Sixpence.' Right. Now they come up with another article. 'Will you give me a pound, sir?' Everybody thinks it's going to be cut price too. Twenty people say, 'Yes', 'Yes', 'Yes' . . . This is the kill. They get these people committed. They've got the boxes there. They haven't given them out yet, but they're taking the pounds. 'Your one, your one, your one . . ' These people had half-expected a reduction. No. And they now begin to dish out the boxes. And the customers have bought a load of rubbish. Another of their strokes is, if they see a real gullible idiot, male or female, in the crowd, they will build up a 'big sell'. They start off with, 'Will you give me 50p for this? And if I give you this, will you make it a pound?' And they'll go on, putting on another box, another article, and asking for more money, until the person is loaded up with boxes. When they think they've taken him for enough, they switch to another potential mug. The happy victim, pleased to be out of the limelight, will quietly walk off. It won't be till he's well away and able to examine his purchases more closely that he'll realize the goods are 'flash'—shoddy, cheaply made, poorly put-together rubbish—he's been took and there's no legal redress. If the police come along in a hurry it's a 'run-out', the Run-Out Merchants have to run away.

The Spieler Albos was a barn of a place where such people could relax.

In spite of the general friendliness, though, some of the jokes the members played on one another were very cruel. One member who'd been a professional fighter in the early twenties—no great art, just a short, squat heavyweight who took his punches and eventually became a taxi driver—he put it about that this other member, about fifteen years older than him and who'd been a PT Sergeant in the First World War and was still slim, fit and strong—he's seventy-two or three now and makes up his own football favours and sells them at the big London clubs—he put it about that he was dead. A couple of months later the dead man turned up and shook everybody by the hand. When he was told what had happened he said to the taxi driver, 'If you fancy coming outside I'll show you what the difference is between your big mouth and me and my dead hand.' The offer wasn't taken up. That trick rebounded. For a couple of bob a man called Smith used to repair watches for club members and their friends. Suddenly the rumour went around—'Smith is dead'. Well, we knew all these jokes so nobody took any notice. About two weeks later, a lady friend of his came in in a temper and screamed, 'Smithy's dead! What a lovely bunch of friends he's got! I told three of you two weeks ago that he was ill in the hospital. He was always doing you good turns in here. He repaired some of your watches for nothing. And not one of you came to see him!'

There was a man called Tony, an ex-railway man in his late sixties. He liked to stroll in with a rolled umbrella, doing the gentleman act, posing, leaning on it and so on. About four or five members decided that they wanted to make him lose his dignity so, when he came in the next time, they grabbed him and went around with him in a mad dance. When men are powerful they can hurt you whether they mean to or not. He went off balance and landed on the floor. Due to a cigarette lighter in his hip pocket he suffered a hairline fracture of the hip and had to go into hospital. When he came out after about three months, he had to use that umbrella as a stick and not for show . . .

Now, all of a sudden, the Gambling Acts were repealed, and I saw members openly playing four-handed rummy with each man putting in half a quid or a pound and whoever won the game pulling the stake less table-money. Punters who used to bet on the snooker games were no longer doing so; they were concentrating their money at better odds on the card games. In such an atmosphere I said to myself, 'I can't go on only having cups of tea and playing the occasional game of snooker.' With a presser named Guss, I began to put dollar bets on the rummy. This was the time when I was beginning to feel the pinch of the loneliness and the bitterness over my so-called friend's villainy and when I was getting nowhere with my singing. I gambled more and more, and not only at The Spieler but also at a club called The Green Dragon in Green Dragon Yard.

I remember when I began to do it really bad. It was a week-end in 1964 or '65, a summer evening. This was the clincher. I'd just been to the pictures at the Mile End Empire with a friend. They played the Queen. I saw a girl who used to go to the Mile End Old Boys' for the dances. It was a Saturday night and I hadn't bothered to have a shave. I said, 'Hello!' She was a nice-looking girl in a big fat way and she gave me a freezing look as if to say, 'I know you, but don't bother about carrying on with the conversation!' It so upset me that, like a drinker who when he's disturbed goes for a drink, when I said goodnight to my friend, I headed straight for The Green Dragon. I saw a friend of mine there, a taxi driver, playing four-handed rummy. I backed him and I won. That was my trouble. I backed him again and again and again, and he won more times than not. I know it sounds silly, but the reason why I didn't play myself was I couldn't shuffle the cards. There's a procedure. It's like when a boxer goes into the ring and he doesn't know how to stand and move around. It shows you up. But I've got the card *sense*. I know that, because I used to look over the shoulders of the players I backed. And I could sprat and I could bluff. Well anyway, I went on backing this friend and, come about half past one, quarter to two, I began to feel a bit tired. I said, 'Sorry, but I've got to go. I'm dead bushed. I've had a hard week.' He said, 'OK, son. Take care of yourself.' I counted when I got home. I think I'd won about thirty pounds. And a win is not good in gambling because if you win it's the set-up to lose.

Because of the trend, I'm now going to the clubs over the week-ends—The Two Aces along the Whitechapel Road, The Dragon Club in the Whitechapel Road, a couple of doors from The Green Dragon, Albos's (very rarely to gamble) and Silver's in Brick Lane. I begin to have a routine—Silver's for Friday evening, Nyman or Massey (the betting shops) Saturday after-noon, Saturday evening The Dragon and, if I've still got money, I go to The Green Dragon on Sunday afternoon and on to The Two Aces till twelve. Though I'm a gambler and I've got the bug, I don't yet gamble from Monday to Thursday as I've got to work five days a week to earn the bread, starting at eight o'clock in the morning.

That was when I was being reasonable. But I began to gamble *all* night Friday, Saturday and Sunday. There was one day it worked out that I was supposed to go in to Beverly Sportswear on a Sunday and I forgot. So about half past seven in the morning when I should be getting out of bed, I'm round the corner from the workshop in The Two Aces having half a quid on someone in a Rummy Final. I lose that half quid. I'm down to about six bob. I haven't slept. I haven't slept all week-end. I go up to the back of the workshop where the lavatories are and I have a cold sluice down and wipe my face and go in to the workshop. I fall asleep during the morning about ten times. Six bob won't last me the week. I ask the Hoffman presser will he help me with a pound, I'm a bit short. I ask the guvnor quietly on the Monday can he lend me a pound. I also borrow another pound from a friend. I'm now able to eat all week until I get paid . . .

Soon I was borrowing at the beginning of the week and paying back at the end of the week and the gambling was going on beyond the week-end. It was not only happening on the Friday, Saturday and Sunday nights, I was also going somewhere on the Monday evenings till one and two o'clock in the morning. I had the stamina of a horse and just as much brains. I was getting more and more involved. In one club I went to, rummy was for the peasants so I played chemmy in a back room.

One week I gambled five nights on the trot without sleep. I would even go from one joint to another on the same night in the middle of the week if the action was slow. I was in real trouble. I was forgetting to pay the rent. I was borrowing a pound or two from a friend, selling a couple of books. I even went halves with people so as to be able to place the minimum bet of half a quid. Time was beginning to lose its importance. The windows and floors of my flat were dirty. My job wasn't life. Gambling was all that mattered.

In 1965 I received a blue Eviction Notice to say I must get out of the Carter House. Then, four weeks after the Council got a Court Order, the Final Notice arrived on a Saturday saying I must be out by Monday morning. I walked into the Spitalfields Market and I said to the watchman, 'Can I borrow a barrow for a pound? I'll bring it back in a couple of hours. I've got to shift some furniture.' Then I went to my sister, by now widowed, in Hunton Court, and told her what had happened. She cried a bit but, being a very practical person, she sent round a couple of her kids to help to shift my china cabinet, my writing bureau (hand-carved by Morry), my oak table, my clothes, photographs, coin collection, books and opera records, my table-model gramophone—as much as we could manage in two journeys—into her back room, where I stayed till 1967 when I found I was happy one day and shouting the next and decided it's one thing to be the kids' visiting uncle and another to be living with them, so I moved to my own room in the Cavell Street.

I must have left about a hundred and twenty of the twelve-inch 78's, mostly orchestral selections, and about four hundred books, behind at the Carter House, including a very large copy with gold painted edges of *Gulliver's Travels* and also *The Book of Josephus*, the Jewish general at the time of Christ who led the Jews in a revolt against the Romans and told them to fight to the last man and then turned up alone, alive and well, afterwards. Thirty-eight years had passed since I first moved into No. 18, the Carter House with my mother, my sister and my five brothers. My mother and Betty used to sleep in the room where my mother had most of her stock. Their window had an iron gate. Me and my brother, Steve, slept in the living-room in a put-you-up which was turned into a sofa by day. Jack slept in the other bedroom in the corner by the window, and Morry slept in the corner, parallel. On the same side as Morry, Alan and Reggie slept feet to feet in a bed near the door. When I woke early on a Saturday morning, I could hear everyone else snoring in different keys to reassure me that I was not alone. And now the last and worst thing that could happen to me had happened. I had lost my home. A young unsullied boy had become a lonely, compulsive gambler who had learned the bitter truths of life—the deceit, the guile and the betrayal . . . It was a sad time, and a sad time should be respected!

Hunton Court, Cavell Street . . . I was still gambling. At the Mile End Old Boys', Boyd Stanger bunged me a fiver and there was talk of raising a collection. They thought I was out of work. I was ashamed and stayed away. Then the club shut down, so did the Old Stepnians'. I had more and more time in which to indulge my vice.

By the second and last week of my fortnight's holiday in June, 1968, I had run through £120 and I hadn't a penny in my pocket. Earlier in the week, standing in The Dragon at one o'clock one morning, I was on a losing streak. I didn't know what to do. The owner of the club came in. We knew one another. He saw me standing there just like a zombie. He gave me a nod and ordered two teas at the bar. He said to me, 'Do you want a cake?', then, not demanding, casual, 'How did it go tonight?' I said, 'Didn't do any good at all.' He said, 'Are you walking out before you go skint?' I said, 'Too late!' He then did something which is not supposed to be in the book. He took out two pound and said, 'You don't owe me this. Put it in your pocket and get out of here and I don't want to see you for a week at least. And when you come back I want you to be ready, I want you to be fresh, I don't want you to be like a beaten dog that's so tired it can't keep its eyes open.' It wasn't generosity. It was pity. And the next afternoon I lost the £2 he gave me in the betting shop.

I hadn't the gall to go into a restaurant and ask for tick. I hung around hoping to meet a friend who'd buy me a meal, till people must have thought I was a suspicious character. At last I met one. I asked him, 'Could you lend me half a quid till pay day so that I can have something to eat?' He said, 'Haven't got it! Haven't got it!' And he was *loaded*! He was working and his wife had inherited money from her mother. I said to myself, 'For five years, Alex, you've been working as a presser solid, and in the middle of your holiday when you should be relaxing, enjoying yourself, you're skint. You've had nothing to eat today, yesterday, and the day before, and to drink you've only had cups of tea indoors. There's the rent to pay and you have the rest of this week to go plus a week back at work before you're paid again. To walk about like this looking for people to borrow from, you must have no pride. You're rubbish. You've lost your manhood.' I could talk to me because I knew me since I was born. I realized I'd come to the end and that I'd got to pull back.

It was the Thursday night. I went into The Green Dragon hoping to meet a taxi driver who'd owed me a pound for about a month. While waiting for him I met another friend, in the building trade, who treated me to a cup of tea and a meal. I must have looked thin and pale for he said, 'What's on your mind?' I told him. He said, 'Well can't you get in touch with your guvnor and ask him for five or six pound? After all, you've been working with him for five years now!'

This is where God or the Devil put his hand in because, that same week, the second week of the holidays, was the week Beverly Sportswear were moving from the back of the building to the front, and the guvnor was going to be there to supervise the lay-out of the workshop and the setting-up of the new tables. So on the Friday, at half past eight o'clock in the morning, as I'm walking along from The Dragon to Cavell Street, I sent up a little bit of a silent prayer: 'Let me tell the one good lie and I'll never lie again!' I worked on the idea as I shaved and cleaned myself up. Then I walked to New Road and into the workshop. I said, 'Pardon me, Guvnor, but could you help me? Could you lend me a fiver so that I can pay the rent and have a couple of pound to go the week because I went to the pictures on Wednesday and I had about twelve pound in my pay packet, just inside beside my tobacco tin, and I pulled out the tin and I must have pulled out the wage packet and it fell to the ground without my noticing.' He believed me, or if he didn't he never said otherwise. He took out a fiver and said, 'Listen! You'll have to pay me back in two weeks. Company money is company money, but this has come out of my own pocket.' I said, 'All right, Guvnor. I'm pleased you've done it for me.' Then I went to Johnnie, the caretaker at Cavell Street, and I said, 'I've had a bit of bad luck this week. Could I owe you a week's money and I'll pay you off a pound of what I owe you every week?' He said, 'OK!'

Every now and then I reckon up the score and, from then on, the idea of gambling was repugnant to me. But I had to defend myself against it. I had to fight me. For what other people take for granted I had to scheme. I had to break a habit which was like eating. I was determined to survive and lift myself out of the dung heap I had pushed myself into. I blessed my mother for her sterling, solid qualities that enabled me to do it. I made myself a silent vow, as sincere as if I had been standing in a synagogue or before my Maker, that I would never let this happen to me again. I said to myself, 'The nights are so long, what shall I do to counterbalance being hooked?' And what I did was buy a Co-op television set from a friend for ten pound and swung to television. With television I was no longer alone. It filled the lonely parts of my existence. It enabled me to eliminate the haphazard moods that caused me to gamble excessively and without reason. My mother once said, and I'll repeat it, 'My television is my window on the world' and I can say as an addict that over the years it has improved. Even the ITV is almost up to standard.

By now I had stopped going to classes at the Smithy Street, due to Miss Whitehead's promotion and the fact that her successor seemed to prefer the ladies to the men. I'd been to one of his classes before and he was reluctant to let me sing 'I'll walk beside you' solo as he was about to start his hour of choral work. He didn't like me upsetting his routine so he gave me haphazard advice on my interpretation. I sang the first verse on a soft melodic line. He said, 'Oh, that's too soft. Sing it louder.' So I sang the second verse louder. He then said, 'What are you singing?! A dramatic aria?!' So I sang the third verse like I sang the first verse. He said nothing, but I had made up my mind and I said to my friend, Alf Hancock, a fellow tenor, 'I don't feel welcome here. Goodnight, Alf!' and I walked out the door and never went back to the classes again. So, in terms of music, I was now a spectator rather than a participant. Luckily there was a wealth of good classical music to enjoy on the television—Mantovani and his orchestra, Eric Robinson and his orchestra in the programme 'Music for You', opera productions such as *Rigoletto, Aida*, and *Carmen*.

But I said to myself, 'You can't cut yourself off from gambling and from people completely. At a time of loneliness you might not only go back to gambling in a big way, you might do something sillier.' So I continued to play the Pools and, come the week-end, as well as watching television and visiting my sister and going on outings to places like Hampton Court and Madame Tussaud's and Regent's Park Zoo with Alma and Adrian, her two younger children, I would do a Yankee at a bookie's—and I still do so, and I'm sometimes lucky.

A Yankee is four horses permutated into six doubles, four trebles and an each-way accumulator. Last January I'd have backed a horse as a single if it hadn't been for someone's mean-mindedness. I'd been going to Staplehurst's, the sweet-shop and newsagent at the corner of the Ford Square, for eighteen months since a new family took over. They seemed friendly people. I took to them. The wife used to tell me any tips she had. I placed a couple of bets for her. He was supposed never to have a bet. Now, one Saturday, he said to me, 'I fancy having a pound on Kingdom.' Kingdom was a sixteen to one outsider. I put on a pound for him and the horse came in first so, after the tax of one pound two pence was paid, he had fifteen pound ninety-eight pence for his pound. Because he never said Kingdom was a tip, I never backed it as a single, I put my money into a Yankee and the other horses got beaten and that was it. 'Well,' I thought, 'I've lost my money on my bet, but a gentleman will give me a pound commission at least. It should be ten per cent, but who's quibbling?' He was never in the shop on Saturdays. I held the money till the Sunday. I went into the shop to get the *Sunday Mirror* and a bar of chocolate. His young girl of eleven or twelve was there. You can't have a man-to-man conversation with a young girl there, particularly as he told me in case he won that I was not to tell the wife. So I give him the money expecting him as a man of the world to give me a pound. He said, 'Have your chocolate on me!' How tight can you get!! Because the kid was there I couldn't say, 'If I want to buy chocolate, I buy it! Be a man and bung me a pound!' I said, 'You can stick your bloody chocolate!' I bought the *Mirror* from his wife on the Monday and I haven't been back. It's not the amount of money involved, it's the principle. I wrote out the bet for him at the bookmakers; I drew the money for him on the Saturday afternoon; I held the money for him till the following day—and he tried to wank me off, he worked a double stroke: he didn't tell me Kingdom was a tip from someone he normally got good tips from and, secondly, he didn't give me a fair commission. So he hasn't only lost a friend, he's lost a customer.

EIGHT

Before I moved in with my sister, I thought her children were the nicest and best behaved children I'd ever met. When I moved out, I was only sorry to leave the dog and the cat.

I've always liked animals. There is in all of them an instinct which recognizes a friend who wishes them no harm. If you treat them like sensible beings they react favourably. I remember in about 1960 or '61 coming home to 18, Carter House and there in the corner of my landing on the ground floor was this little bundle of fur. I said Hello to it and it miaowed. It was a beautiful tortoiseshell cat. Her claws had been removed so she was probably a show cat that had run away from a very hard master or mistress. She had deep blue eyes and her fur was ginger and brown. Mr Pini, who had a restaurant at the corner of Hanbury Street and Commercial Street, didn't have any cats so I thought, 'I'll take her to him.' I forgot one thing: he was Italian, and any animal which isn't useful is not considered by the Italians to be good. A dog must keep away people, a cat kill mice, a cow give milk—there's no sentimentality in Italians like there is in the English, the Jewish, and the Irish and the rest who make up this mad island of ours. We like animals for their company, but the Italians are a very practical people. I took Mr Pini this cat. I really regretted it afterwards. He put her down in the basement on her own with plenty to eat. She was supposed to keep down the rats and the mice. After about two or three months he said to me, 'Do you mind taking back that cat?' I said, 'Why?' He said, 'She's weeing herself all over the food and the corn and the other stuff we store down below.' I took her back. Of course she was weeing! She was weeing because she was a very unhappy cat, like a child wees the bed when it's unhappy. She was receiving no affection. I took her round to my sister. There she would be in a house of love with other cats. She wee-ed all over the place to begin with, then gradually settled down and in time gave birth to Horace who had a hump and a slump in the back but nevertheless married another cat and the family perpetuated itself.

Another experience with a cat was when I went to keep an appointment with Domb's, the dentist in the Whitechapel Road. I'd a sore nose and a thick head, the results of a raging cold. I sat down in the waiting-room. There was a little black cat with golden eyes on the next seat. After a while somebody else took a seat, somebody else, somebody else, and the place began to fill up. The cat hopped onto my lap. I gave her a stroke. She crawled up my chest and was hanging over my shoulder like a baby who wants to relieve the hiccoughs. Then she climbed onto my head. I said, 'No claws, please!' She sat there for about half an hour, no claws. I was sitting quite still. Everybody was laughing. Come my turn, I gently took her off and gave her a stroke and I never saw that cat again. Neither did I see my cold again. Cats like to sit on something warm like a wireless set. When she went up onto my head, my head was burning. By the time I saw the dentist she had taken all the heat and fever out of it, my cold was cured and the old brain was ticking away on all cylinders.

As regards dogs, I was once walking down a long road and I saw a little puppy galloping as hard as it could out of a courtway. It got to a door, went, 'Yip! Yip!', the door opened and he dived in. Just a minute later a big powerful dog came dashing in pursuit, stopped at the door, and for about five minutes he was outside that door woof-woofing. Another dog I knew used to guard a door and, when anybody knocked, he used to roar till the door shook, yet he was only a dachshund playing a part and, as soon as he realized you were a friend, he wanted you to stroke him and talk. These are the sort of signs which show animals have intelligence and human qualities.

The greatest woman apart from my mother that I ever knew was my sister's dog, Lulu. She was part alsatian, part golden labrador. Though she had about a dozen suitors, she had twenty-nine puppies by her husband elect—Ginger, an Irish wolfhound—and by no one else. If an actress had the eyes of Lulu, she wouldn't have to say a word. When I brought home some fish I felt almost a mental impulse to give in to those big brown eyes and say, 'Go on, Lulu! Have it!' I had to say, 'Go away, Lulu! Don't look at me! Lulu, go away!' She was so intelligent, she was a person. Never mind the fact that she could only bark—she could communicate. Once she was given an order by my sister: 'Take the children over to the park and see that they don't go away!' Antoinette was a rebel, she tried to break away, but Lulu grabbed her dress and dragged her back. My sister soon came to recognize that she'd got another woman in the house—a loyal, devoted woman. And what a sexy one! From the front she looked very big and strong, which she was, but, if you walked behind her, you saw very nicely curved back legs, which were slender at the calf, and a very tantalizing bottom—she didn't wag her tail to greet you like other dogs, she wagged that tantalizing bottom! She once showed her love and obedience to me beyond all question. During her heat period she was surrounded by six or seven dogs. My sister, who goes sailing through life unaware of the seasons of the love-life of dogs, said, 'Alex! Call Lulu in!' I opened the door and roared, 'Lulu!' Lulu broke away from her admirers and came trotting up. She used to try to climb into bed with me but I said No. She accepted it. Instead she had a little trick. I used to leave the bedroom door open and lie with my hand protruding over the bed and, early morning, she'd come marching in and have her back stroked, without me doing anything, by going backwards and forwards underneath my hand.

Though she was a very intelligent dog, she had a 'thing' to begin with about cats. When she was about six months old she killed three within a week. No cat ever came down Hunton Court again while she was there. But in the house was always a cat. The latest was Minnie. She was never strong. Even her kittens died. But she was clever. She made sure she was on top of the wardrobe when she heard the heavy paws of Lulu approaching. When Lulu had her first litter of nine pups, she didn't know what to do with them. Minnie had learned from her mother what to do. While Lulu rested on the sack, Minnie licked the eyes of the little puppies and, from that time on, Lulu and she were bosom friends.

Greed was Lulu's only weakness. She used her eyes to charm the food off the plates. It was nothing to see my young nephews and nieces slipping a potato or a bit of meat underneath the table for her to snaffle—and they weren't given enormous helpings for themselves. A boy, once, was on the pavement, sucking an ice-lolly. Lulu walked out the door, took one look, and, with a nudge of her shoulder, knocked the lollipop out of the boy's hand and began to lick it up. The boy started bawling, and my sister had to buy him another lolly and drag Lulu inside. And, one Friday, Lulu knew she was going to have a hard time with her next litter so, with her paw, she worked open the door of the larder and ate four to four and a half pound of roast lamb. Nothing was left but the bare bone. My sister made a profit, though, because she sold the puppies at ten bob a time. Some neighbours knew of Lulu's weakness and put poisoned meat in their bin and that was the end of Lulu.

I'll never forget our daily routine. When I came home in the evening, the kids sat around on chairs with maybe one or two on the couch along with Lulu and Minnie beside her, and I'd sit in the big armchair and share out sweets with the kids and Lulu (Minnie didn't like them) while we all watched television. Give a sherbet lemon to Lulu and—crunch!—it was away! Same with chocolates and liquorice all-sorts—I used to share them out and she was one of the family. Once, because she'd worms, I said, 'I'm sorry, Lulu! No chocolates!' She drooped her eyes and looked very sad and all the children said, 'Go on, Uncle! Give her one! Give her one!' 'All right!' I said, 'I'm under pressure. All right!' As I said it, and before I'd even taken the piece of chocolate out of the bag, her eyes lit up again and she was happy.

There's a postscript. I've seen the spirit of my brother Jack—big fat rosy cheeks, brown suit, double size and smiling. I've seen the spirit of Jack's father, his face covered in a golden blaze. I've seen the spirit of my mother. But I don't know if anyone else has ever seen the shade of a dog lying on their bed as Lulu did on mine in Cavell Street about two or three nights after I was told she died.

I've often wondered if Tiddles, Betty's present cat, is haunted by the spirit of Lulu. He's a prime cat, full of randiness. He's black with a bit of ginger and he's powerfully built and uncommonly handsome with a high forehead, well-defined shoulders and claws more than an inch long. My sister says, 'But Lulu was a dog,' and I say, 'Species has nothing to do with the spirit.'

The people who don't believe in spirits are the people who've never come into contact with them. During the war my sister had to go into a Home in Epsom because she wouldn't eat and she kept thinking she saw Myer Bergwein, the window repairer of our childhood, looking at her through a trap-door in the ceiling and telling her that this life was no good and she should join him. Her husband told me the only way to get rid of this spirit haunting her was to burn two photographs she had of Myer Bergwein and throw out his bag of diamond cutters. I did just that. Then, the same night in bed, I heard this voice in my mind saying, 'Where's my tools?!' I felt the presence. I felt it come closer. It came so close I reached up and I grabbed where the neck might be and I concentrated and I squeezed and I slung the presence through the wall. I used up so much nervous energy I couldn't move for about a half hour. I was petrified, not in fear but because all the energy had been drained out of me. From then on my sister became more reasonable and Myer Bergwein never came back into her life or mine, and she began to eat again and she recovered. Within a month she was discharged. She had put on weight and was no longer haunted, but I never told her why.

At one time, the terrace I live in in Cavell Street was called the Guvnors' Houses. The guvnors lived with their families and had their workshops there. I woke up one night in 1970 and saw a giant friendly and cuddly teddy-bear, about six foot tall, moving its arms and its head. As I looked, it reduced its size to the height of the leg of the chair. I looked again and in its place was a tiger, not a genuine Bengal tiger but a toy tiger eighteen inches to two feet high. All of a sudden there appeared instead a woman of fifty-five to sixty but in good trim, dressed as a circus performer in pseudo-military uniform. I smiled. She smiled and bowed. Then I went back to sleep.

At 46, Cavell Street, I've got the smallest room in the building apart from the lavatory. I could walk round it in six paces. There's a bed and, at the back of it near the door, a gas stove, a battered old thing with a broken oven and grill but which I can use to fry and boil, and which has a cone heater attached. Between the bed and the stove there's a chest of drawers which I eat off and where I keep my crockery. I've two wardrobes and, apart from my own chair, two chairs I put books on—Westerns mostly. Just after the war I received a gift of an American soft-back issued to the American troops about the history of the Civil War. Because of that, I began to acquire a lot of true-life books about the Outlaws, the Marshals and the Indian Raids. I made a bit of a collection and I've still got it. The television set is on a dressing-table at the head of the bed. If a friend comes in he has to sit on the bed. Just outside my door on the left hand side there's the lavatory and on the right hand side there's the sink with cold and colder water. The building, along with the whole row, is under a Compulsory Purchase Order, so all the tenants, including me, will have to get bachelor flats in compensation. For six years I used to entertain a Yiddisher boy who lived two floors below. He was ill. He was a gambler. At week-ends I let him watch boxing on my television and if there was any surplus food I gave it to him. If he was in a bit of trouble he could leave his suitcase with me. He knew I was a friend and could depend on it. All of a sudden, after six years, he's up in my room and I tell him I've £1,500 invested in Unit Trust shares. That burned him in the gull. He said, 'I hope they don't re-house you!' I was looking at him. He repeated it: 'I hope they don't re-house you!' I told him he'd better eff off, and that was the last time I spoke to him. He's a stupid emotional person. What he said was like a curse. He's a victim of the benevolent society. While the rest of us put the effort in, he talks of a Utopia where there's no rich people and there's no poor people, yet he's been a parasite on this country for at least twelve years and gets seven and a half quid for food and three pounds for his rent from the National Assistance. That I work and save and plan got right up the nose of that greedy, lazy, poncing dreck.

When first I went to Cavell Street I used to make soup.

I'd half a dozen people coming in for a chunk of bread and some of my famous soup. I had a magic formula. I bought potatoes, carrots and onions and tins of baked and butter beans. I boiled the potatoes and onions for twenty minutes and the carrots for twenty-five. Then I added the baked and butter beans and, to all that, I added a tin of chicken soup and a tin of vegetable soup and kept turning, turning them as they simmered on a low gas till any yellow glutamen had dissolved. I seasoned it with salt and black pepper and added more water till I had about a gallon of soup, enough for six people on the Saturday and Sunday. The smell! Everybody in the house knew whose soup it was. Two of my free-loading friends rowed with one another on one of my soup nights. One said to me, 'If he's coming in, I'm not coming in!' The other said to me, 'If he's coming in, I'm not coming in!' Yet when I blew out the two of them, they ended up all palsy-walsy chatting to one another and neither of them speaking to *me*! Friendship though it's solid is intangible, and though it's the strongest tie that people can have it's also extremely delicate. That might sound a paradox but it's true.

After supper, one Tuesday evening in March or April of 1973, I don't know why but I was feeling particularly happy. I bought a couple of packets of biscuits from Sylvie, a local shopkeeper, cracked a few jokes and said, 'I'd better go home now and make myself a cup of tea and have a few biscuits and watch the telly.' I went upstairs to my room. The lock was on but open. I said to myself, 'Hullo! Didn't I lock it?!' When I opened the door, the place looked as though a gang of navvies had walked in and turned it over. This is what was missing, and I believe it was a person who'd drunk my soup that did the job: £40 in five pound notes from under the mattress, £30 in face value of pre-1946 silver coins (including George VI's, George V's, a couple of Edwards and a few Victorias), and also two pounds of sugar, quarter of a pound of tea, half a bottle of cognac in a special French box, a few bars of chocolate and some sherbet lemons. He, she or it also stole my Post Office Book. It took me three hours to clean up and find out what was missing. I made a vow that I wouldn't leave any papers or anything of value there any more. So now I carry on me my birth certificate, my parents' marriage lines and my Post Office Book. And my Burial Society Book—when I die I want to go down in the proper place; if God wants to burn me afterwards that's His business, I don't want to burn twice. You naturally assume people never rob friends. But it had happened before with Jerry, a friend since schooldays. Now it was a person who'd drunk my soup. As I'd already had cause to learn, friendships can be betrayed.

Maybe people become your friends because they're lonely. There's one so-called friend of mine at Cavell Street who lived with me on and off at the Carter House and once worked with me as a tailor's hand for three months before I settled down with Beverly Sportswear. I've mentioned him before. His name is Lionel. He's a pent-up person who lives on his nerves. He's six foot and weighs fourteen stone, he looks a big boy. You would have thought a man so solid would have a definite purpose in life. No. He's a good worker yet he hasn't got belief in himself. He vies with people working at the same job to prove that he's as good as them or he's quicker than them, which is a pepping-up of the morale that I don't go with. I go to the workshop with one principle—to clear the work on my table. There's only a few people in the shop who can make me shout and one of them's the tailor. He's a Polish Jew who doesn't seem to work. He organizes. He puts on a performance. When I can't bottle up my feelings I shout at him blue murder and I feel better. But Lionel can't do a thing like that. So how's he going to relieve himself? Is he going to beat somebody up? Is he going to rape a woman? No. He's going to let it out on friends, and that's why he hasn't got too many. He can be the nicest person in the world and, for no apparent reason, completely change his personality over night. One Thursday at the Carter House he said to me after I'd repaid him ten bob a day earlier than I need have, 'You can borrow money from me any time. You're a good boy.' Right. But Friday morning he says, 'Why don't you get up, you big fat-gutted git?!' Those were the words that greeted me! He fancied having a row. So he went away for two or three weeks, then came back and apologized. That was one of the eight or nine times he left me. The man couldn't throw off his tensions in any other way. I know his problem. Yet I don't talk to him about it because if you try to help him that upsets him too. I once tried. I said, 'Lionel, I work with you. You're a good worker. What are you keying yourself up for? You're a big man. A big man doesn't work fast. Do your work at a nice natural pace.' He seemed to agree with me but he remained a grouchy old bear just the same.

Talking about relieving tensions, I'd a row with the Hoffman presser at the workshop in the February of that very heavy winter in 1969, on the Thursday before the snow and ice completely vanished. I walked out in a temper and, just to give me the rub in and to show they had not forgiven me for never becoming a chazzen, the spirits made me slip on the ice as I came back from dinner. I lay on the pavement with two ligaments sticking about an inch and a quarter out of one of my knees. I gave a shout, 'For God's sake, somebody help me to get up!' Four men did so, after which I struggled on my own to the London Hospital for treatment. I had thought that at last I had grown up and changed my ways and had defeated the spirits which had tried to put me down and keep me there, and now, with my dislocated knee, I was an old man for the next two years.

I won through, though, with new facets added to my nature. I was less selfish. I sympathized with those who were crippled or otherwise afflicted. I was more tolerant. I thought of people beyond friends and family. My mind had been strengthened; my eyes were opened up to two more realities of life—that people are frail and there but for the grace of God go I.

But the spirits hadn't finished with me yet. After crippling me for two years, they intended to show me that however bad things are they can get worse.

On the Monday before Easter last, I was working at the bench and day-dreaming, 'Why the hell can't I win the Pools! This is just the survival stakes. I want to start living and set up a nice home for my sister and her kids in or near Brighton, and go into business for myself instead of working with the iron and having the guvnor coming in all the time and telling me to stop talking. I'd open up a shop called "The Winter Sunshine Shop" and I'd sell tinned fruits and real fruits and salmon and trussed chickens ready for eating from the fridge. I'd go around

Brighton and Reading and Luton looking for nice little paintings—not pictures you've to puzzle out, and they needn't be with anybody's name. I'd also buy pottery and china, and I'd buy two record players—a modern one with a couple of speakers, and an old type that you wind up which would have to have a wooden box because wood makes a beautiful sound. I'd begin to accumulate records again like "The Golden Treasury of Immortal Performers" and "Memories of the Metropolitan". I'd like to go to La Scala, Milan, and the New Metropolitan to see how it compares with the Old. I'd have a garden with flower beds—not just a lawn—and a rock garden and a few trees and a pool with goldfish . . .' I was getting a bit impatient, in other words, with my slowness in acquiring wealth! My mind then moved on to the effect of the General Election and the Tories losing their majority but Labour not getting a large majority either. I was going to make some comment to Ziggy, my fellow under presser who was about six feet away from me on my left side, when I was surprised to find that my mouth was curved round to talk to him though I hadn't moved my head. I knew that I was sweating on the back of the head and that the draught was hitting me from the window behind, and I'd heard of neuralgia, but I'd never heard of this. By the Wednesday my right eye had bunged up too and was weeping, while I had an arch to my left eyebrow like it was surprised. The left side of my face was alive, laughing, talking. The other side was in mourning. I consulted the doctor and he said I'd Bell's Palsy. He recommended Disprin for the cold and, for the palsy, he said I should wait until the cold went away before he decided what to do. By instinct I massaged the muscles of the side of the face and neck, and I twitched my eyebrows and blew raspberries and whistled with my mouth to remind them of their duties. The only trouble was I couldn't blow raspberries and I couldn't whistle! But I healed myself in two months.

Some spirits are good, some bad, some indifferent. The bad ones I'm still fighting, but I remember my father when he was an old man talking about his uncles—the governor of a Dutch island, a doctor, the story teller I've mentioned who was given a small title . . . Now I'm not going to say that the spirits of these people have come into me as the singing one did, but I do feel that they occasionally direct me at times of crisis. Take medicine, for instance—and I'm not talking about pulling out a tooth or doing a complicated operation. Though I haven't received any training or read any books on the subject, it's as though the spirit of one of my ancestors who was a doctor was sometimes guiding me.

When I was about thirteen years old and a member of the Habonim, we went one Sunday in June for a hike into the country. I didn't have too good a pair of shoes because I was a growing boy and there was a habit in my family of older brothers passing down their shoes and suits to me. Anyway, I had this pair of shoes which was size nine. The fact that my feet were size ten was beside the point. They were very nice, they were black, and I was to go on this ramble, so on this Sunday morning I put on this pair of black shoes and the rest of my clean clobber. I had six suits to choose from, don't forget, so I picked out a grey one with a white shirt and I joined the members of the Habonim of the Joseph Trumpeldor Group and we took a coach for a shilling to the outskirts of London and walked all over Kent, exploring it to the extreme. During the time I was walking, and it was a very hot day as it had that habit in June, I noticed a bit of irritation in my left big toe. Well, boys aren't supposed to be cry-babies and it wasn't too painful at the beginning, but as the day went on it was hurting more and more, and I don't mind telling that towards four or five, when we were thinking of getting back to where we lived, I began to limp. I limped home from Aldgate Coach Station. I let myself in and, as soon as I could, I took off my shoe and sock and I saw something that by description might sound rather painful but, as I looked at it, I found I was looking at it with the eyes of a doctor and could forget the pain. I saw on my big toe an area of about three-eighths of an inch in diameter which was dull yellow. Right away I knew exactly what to do. If anybody asked me now exactly how and why I knew, all I could say is that whoever was a doctor in my family in the bygone days, he was doing the directing. I selected a pair of nail-cutters with very sharp points. I also found an old shirt and I tore off a couple of rough clean bandages. I went into the kitchen and I lit the gas and I very quickly passed the scissors over it. Then, very cold-bloodedly, I nipped a corner of where the yellow part of my toe was and I began to squeeze. I squeezed out all the pus. I squeezed out all the liquid below it which was almost like water. Then I got to the blood and I made sure I squeezed a lot of that and all. That left a nice little hole. I didn't cut off the dead skin because somehow something in my mind said the dead skin was going to drop off of its own accord after giving a bit of protection. I bandaged the toe up and I put on a pair of slippers. The next morning when I looked, the hole was beginning to fill up, and within a week you couldn't tell there had been anything the matter.

My brother, Alan, who used to sleep over Saturday night at the 18 Carter House so as to be able to sell salad stuff in the Lane next day, said to me as he came through the door one evening in 1953 or '54, 'I've got trouble!' He showed me his forearm. It was all puffed up. On the Friday he'd had a boil on the middle finger of his left hand. His wife had applied pressure to the head of it so it broke away, went underneath the skin and became the worst thing of the lot, which is a wandering or a blind boil. His forearm was now twice as thick as normal and the only sign that he had a boil there was a dull red patch about an inch in diameter. I squeezed and squeezed. The patch opened. The protecting water came out and I could see very gradually, as the hole was opening up, a little bit of creamy white. It couldn't escape me because I was working from the wrist to the crook of the arm; I was closing in, closing in. I got it out. It was three-quarters of an inch long and the thickest part was three-eighths of an inch solid matter, jelly-like. Out it came—Pop! I squeezed, I squeezed. I got water. Then came the blood. My brother was oh-ing in agony. I said, 'Right, Alan! Now comes the painful part!' I got hold of a bowl. I filled it up with warmish water and I put in half a handful of sour salt. I made him put his elbow in it and then, after about five minutes, I let him off the hook and I dried his arm and put on a loose bandage and, in the morning, the wound was beginning to heal up.

After the war I became very friendly with this man Stanley Jackson and his wife Frances and his two brothers-in-law and his mother- and father-in-law, Mr and Mrs Jack Gevelb—I tell you, I was friends with the whole family. About 1950/51, on a bit of a cold winter's night, I went round to see them. Suddenly Stanley gave a little bit of a moan. I said, 'What's the matter, Stanley?' He said, 'This thumb of mine which I dislocated a couple of years ago, it gives me twinges in the winter-time.' I looked at it and I said, 'Show me both your hands so that I can see exactly where the dislocation is.' He showed me both his hands and I noticed that the top part of the thumb that had been twisted was thick and slightly askew. I said, 'Stanley, I won't hurt you but I'll put your thumb back again in its socket. It'll probably take a couple of days before you can use it again properly.' There was no panic or fear on his part. He just assumed that I knew what I was doing and, frankly, I wondered if I did or whether I was being directed. I took hold of the thumb and I pulled the top away from the centre and I turned it slightly so that it conformed with the shape of the other thumb. Then I let it go and it went back into its socket. There was no pain. He said, 'Should I put on any bandage?' I said, 'No.' He still couldn't manipulate it. It was like he was wearing a splint. Within a couple of days it was beginning to move, it had more life. Thank you. It was accepted that I had the talent of a bone-setter. What happens next? His father-in-law is lying in bed. All of a sudden he's twisted a tendon in the back. When next I call he's lying in a big armchair and, every half hour, while we're talking, his wife is bringing him hot water bottles and she's putting them underneath his back and he's saying, 'Oh!' and he's making faces and he's in pain. I said, 'I'll try to ease it for you.' I put some cream he gave me onto the spot where the pain was, which was half way between one shoulder and the lumbar region, and began very, very gently to do a little simple movement with my hands. But the hot water bottle had made his skin so tender that it began to come off. I said, 'Pardon me, Mr Gevelb, but this is no good for you.' Then suddenly something happened. I thought to myself, 'The pain is caused by a tensing up of the muscles which are trying to protect him from the pain. In other words, the pain is caused by the muscles trying to stop the pain.' I said to him, 'I can't massage you, but I'll give you a gentle vibration. I'll put one hand on top of your shoulder where your shoulder-blade is and I'll put the other near the lumbar region and I'll do a vibratory movement to make the muscles relax.' No Boom Boom, just the left hand to the shoulder-blade and the right to the lumbar in repeated movements. To my surprise, in about five minutes he said, 'Ah, that's marvellous! The pain's gone!' And I was only trying to relieve it!

Another time, when Mr Gevelb had a slipped disk—long before they stretched people's spines on large tables—I told him to put his arms around my shoulders. I then bent down as if I was a horse. I said, 'As I straighten up, I want you to imagine that your feet are carrying fourteen pound of iron each.' As I straightened up, I stretched his spine. He said, 'Marvellous! You've eased it!'

In all these cases I knew exactly what to do though I was not a doctor—which ties in with my idea that spirits influence events and make them happen. God sees the universe and us as swirling flecks floating round and round in a brandy glass. He can't look in detail at any particular world though, perhaps, through His spirits, He knows how we are progressing. I believe in God devoutly, though He writes a very complicated script and He's asleep most of the time and He lets some bad things happen. I've met in my life Jewish and Christian people who have lost their belief in God. They point, for instance, to the Nazi atrocities. My answer has always been, 'Don't blame God. He has too much confidence in our ability to raise ourselves above evil and the human condition, and He didn't believe those things would happen.'

In view of the spirit world, I doubt if there is much I could have done to change the way things went. It's as though we were being observed and controlled from UFO's in outer space. The spirits hear what we think, see what we do and, in my case, because I wanted to be a singer and not a chazzen, because I wanted to do it my way, they denied me the trappings of fame and fortune. 'Be a good singer, but don't get paid for it!' 'Do a lot of singing, but work in a workshop like a donkey!'

But there's a satisfaction that goes beyond fame and money. Oh, I didn't sing to those audiences of millions on radio or on television. But I did sing to large audiences at the Troxy and at the Poplar Civic, I did sing in G and S operas, I did sing all over London, sometimes two to three times a week, in countless charity and benefit shows whenever and wherever the opportunity arose, and wherever I sang I hardly ever died the death or, as the Americans say, I was hardly ever a cold turkey. I did the thing I most wanted to do, that I was born for, that I could almost do without bread for—singing old songs as if they were new and letting the people who were listening to me discover the lyrics and melodies of the English ballads and appreciate the feeling of the Italian arias sung in a good translation with the art of an Italian singer.

Most people have to accept that they will not achieve what they think is their right mode of living. In Show Business, you've got to have someone who can direct you and the right people seeing you and pushing you and advising you and advising others to see you and to use you. Otherwise too much is against you. So I don't consider I've failed. You can only fail if you've been there and muffed it. When you're on the side-lines and you're ready to go on and waiting to go on yet you don't get a fair chance to get on that stage and make a name for yourself, I don't think it's real failure. It's a case of it didn't happen.

Looking back on a life full of promise which didn't become fulfilled, I have no regrets because, although I didn't make a success of it, I enjoyed the company, the excitement and the endeavour. Even the disappointments made life interesting. Over the years I have acquired a lot of knowledge and a number of very good friends such as Boyd Stanger who, like people on cue, when the ashes of my ambition began to flicker and die, revived the flame so that I could try again. Fame and wealth and all the good things that come from them just weren't in the cards. But there was always hope and something to keep my interest, keep me going over long and sometimes dreary weeks of work. There was always the pleasure of anticipation. Better luck the next time around!